A Bucket of Eels & The Modern Husband

This volume brings together two provocative and experimental dramas revolving around marriage and coupling.

First seen in Stratford as part of the 1994 Royal Shakespeare Company Festival, *A Bucket of Eels* is a skilful contemporary farce. The action follows ⬚⬚⬚⬚⬚⬚⬚⬚⬚⬚⬚⬚⬚⬚⬚⬚⬚⬚⬚⬚ events, unleashed when ⬚⬚⬚⬚⬚⬚⬚⬚⬚⬚⬚⬚⬚⬚⬚⬚⬚⬚⬚⬚ of his marriage.

The Modern Husband, after ⬚⬚⬚⬚⬚⬚⬚⬚⬚⬚⬚⬚⬚⬚⬚ Henry Fielding, depicts a ⬚⬚⬚⬚⬚⬚⬚⬚⬚⬚⬚⬚⬚⬚ ge vows are openly subordin⬚⬚⬚⬚⬚⬚⬚⬚⬚⬚⬚⬚⬚⬚ and sexual gratification. The play was toured nationally by the Actors Touring Company in 1995.

Paul Godfrey was born in the West Country. He trained and worked as a director in Scotland between 1982 and 1987. His work includes: *Inventing a New Colour* (Royal Court, 1988); *Once in a While the Odd Thing Happens* (Royal National Theatre, 1990); *A Bucket of Eels* (RSC Festival, 1994); *The Panic* (ROH Garden Venture, 1991); *The Blue Ball* (Royal National Theatre, 1995) and *The Modern Husband* (Actors Touring Company, 1995).

by the same author

Once in a While the Odd Thing Happens
The Blue Ball

Paul Godfrey

A Bucket of Eels & The Modern Husband

Introduced by the author

Methuen Drama

Methuen Modern Plays

First published in Great Britain 1995
by Methuen Drama
an imprint of Reed Consumer Books Ltd
Michelin House, 81 Fulham Road, London SW3 6RB
and Auckland, Melbourne, Singapore and Toronto
and distributed in the United States of America
by Heinemann, a division of Reed Elsevier Inc
361 Hanover Street, Portsmouth, New Hampshire
NH 03801 3959

A Bucket of Eels copyright © 1995 by Paul Godfrey
The Modern Husband copyright © 1995 by Paul Godfrey
Foreword copyright © 1995 by Paul Godfrey
The author has asserted his moral rights

ISBN 0–413–688305

A CIP catalogue record for this book
is available from the British Library

Typeset by Wilmaset Ltd, Birkenhead, Wirral
Printed and bound in Great Britain
by Cox and Wyman Ltd, Reading, Berks.

Caution

Contents

Foreword

Perhaps everyone has a few years in their life when all their pals who are going to be married get married? These plays span those years in my life.

I wrote them five years apart and it was only when both existed, complete, that I discovered the connection. *A Bucket of Eels* was written in 1987–8 and by the time I wrote *The Modern Husband* in 1993–4 I had forgotten the earlier play.

Yet the two plays do complement each other and I hope the reader will enjoy a lively contrast in reading both. For as much as these plays connect, they exist independently too; since what links both plays can't be said to describe the subject of either one.

Both dramas revolve around coupling and marriage. As a playwright I perceive the world through dialogue, I am aware that couples are the links that construct a society and consequently the stresses of a society are visible as tension between couples.

Couples, pairs and twins are essentials in drama. Each of these plays has at least one pair of characters who are linked through opposing beliefs. The twins Julia and Ralph live civilised and pagan lives respectively. Mrs Modern chooses to be promiscuous and Mrs Bellamant is monogamous of choice.

But no choice can ever be reduced to just either/or, and in spite of the pairs I've outlined there's little that's systematic in either play. The makings and breakings of couples that take place in each drama trace the successes and failures of people as they negotiate the possibilities available to them. Seen personally the possibilities of life remain infinite while socially they can be pitifully limited. All these characters strain to reconcile their desires.

In drama you explore the ambiguity of experience. An actor's response to a playwright's words and an audience's reception of that in a moment has the potential to transcend the reductive languages that we use to describe ourselves as people.

The need to couple and the desire for a sympathetic union

confront us with our instincts, our language and our society. The choices that we make, reflecting the nature of our instincts and the options we discover as a result, outline the drama of our lives for each one of us.

Every reader or member of the audience will have a different relationship to these plays but I hope all will find enough that they *recognise*.

Paul Godfrey
Clerkenwell, 1995

A Bucket of Eels

For Polly

Every doubt that sings
All the questions that we find
Everything anyone feels
Untidy experience of things
The flickers in your mind
It's all a bucket of eels.

Characters

Mrs Sparrow, *an old postmistress*
Nick, *a trainee manager*
April, *a free spirit*
Julia, *Ralph's sister*
Ralph, *Julia's brother*
Stella, *unemployed*

The action takes place on one night in a forest in Britain, before the end of this century.

A Bucket of Eels was first performed on 14 January 1994 in a production without décor at the Buzz Goodbody Studio, RSC, The Other Place, Stratford-upon-Avon, with the following cast:

Mrs Sparrow	Ali Troughton
Nick	Simon Coury
April	Sian Radinger
Julia	Caroline Payne
Ralph	Stephen Simms
Stella	Helen Franklin

Directed by Claire Nielson

Setting

The most convincing recreation of a wood possible on stage; beech trees, plenty of undergrowth, bracken, brambles and nettles. Real turf and leaves. The fragrance of damp turf and leaf-mould brought into the theatre.

The play is set in a clearing, at least three entrances are necessary, also the facility to jump from a tree.

Firework

The firework, 'A Mine of Serpents', in Act Four, fires wriggling snakes of light into the air. It is manufactured by Standard Fireworks Ltd, Crossland Hill, Huddersfield, West Yorks, (0484) 640640.

The variant texts on pages 72–3 are to cover the variables introduced by the use of a real firework. If fire regulations prevent this entirely then a dramatic convention to represent the firework can be found.

Act One

In the woods, dusk. **Mrs Sparrow** *and* **Nick** *talking.* **Nick** *wears a cheap suit.*

Mrs Sparrow
An undeserved present is the best.
Like this summer;
I've not worked for it.

Nick
But it's been terrible, a bad summer.

Mrs Sparrow
Today was warm.

Nick
Was that it, the summer then, one day?
Some present.

Mrs Sparrow
It was a welcome present, today.

Nick
I've worked for it you know.
Just today; one day: it's not enough.
We deserve a better present than this.

Mrs Sparrow
I'm not talking about what we deserve, but what we get.

Nick
The woods have grown so thick,
I'd like to lie down in the leaves and die.

Mrs Sparrow
And spoil your lovely suit?
Besides it could be better tomorrow.

Nick
I don't mind. I wouldn't know if I wasn't here.

Mrs Sparrow
Yes, but if you were, you'd be glad not to have missed it.

Nick
You're right. I had hoped for good weather tomorrow.

Mrs Sparrow
You get married tomorrow.

Nick
I was going to get married tomorrow.

Mrs Sparrow
You were?

Nick
I was.

Mrs Sparrow
You was?

Nick
I'm not now, not at all.

Mrs Sparrow
Oh.

Nick
And all the presents . . .

Mrs Sparrow
. . . undeserved.

Nick
It's lucky I met you, the Postmistress.

Mrs Sparrow
I often come out here for a couple of hours.
I watch the cars on the road.

Nick
Do you think you could take a note?
It needs to get there tomorrow.

He gives her the note.

This explains that I've left and won't be back.
I'm going to spend the night to think
and in the morning I'll be gone.

Mrs Sparrow
You will wait until tomorrow, won't you?

Nick
Why?

Mrs Sparrow
Because anything could happen on the shortest night.

Nick
Before the longest day . . .

Mrs Sparrow
You're very certain.

Nick
I made up my mind.

Mrs Sparrow
What lovely writing you have.

Nick
My fountain pen. God I thought I lost it today,
I was really upset, till I found it again.

Mrs Sparrow
Nick. That's your name, isn't it?

Nick
There's no postcode on it, I'm afraid.
Perhaps you know the postcode?

Mrs Sparrow
There aren't any postcodes round here.

Nick
That's good. I like that. See you later, perhaps.

He goes.

Mrs Sparrow (*aside*)
No postcode?
No stamp!
Why should I do this?
I didn't think.
A lovelorn wood wanderer.

Enter **April**. *She has a stick.*

Mrs Sparrow
Hello.

April
Do you believe in magic?

Mrs Sparrow
When I shut my front door this evening
all the street lamps went on.

April
Often I wake up just seconds before my alarm clock goes off.

Mrs Sparrow
But I do that. It's not magic.

April
Not magic, but all magic is.

Mrs Sparrow
This magic it's not so special is it?

April
I'm not going to use an alarm clock any more.

Mrs Sparrow
Rise with the sun?

April
I want to wake up in the morning on my own.

Mrs Sparrow
I've been doing it for years, and got into the habit.
Since the clock stopped in the Post Office
I simply get on with everything.

I find more happens now.

April
Do you grow your own food too?

Mrs Sparrow
I don't have need of anything.

April
Self-sufficient then?

Mrs Sparrow
No, I have many friends.

April
I have these four-leafed clovers.

Mrs Sparrow
Are you expecting something to happen?

April
Anything.

Mrs Sparrow
And the stick?

April
That's something else.

Mrs Sparrow
Are you lost?

April
I'm glad you've talked to me.
It's what I like about it here:
people are not strangers to each other.

Mrs Sparrow
But I don't know you!

Enter **Julia**. *She holds up an apple.*

Julia
Look what someone gave me?

April
An apple.

Julia
My best wedding present.

Mrs Sparrow
Then I should eat it if I were you.

Julia
It's far too nice to eat.
But what else can a woman do with an apple?

April
You could plant it somewhere.

Mrs Sparrow
Julia this is. . . ?

April
April.

Julia
I'll call my first child April!

April
Why not May or June?

Mrs Sparrow
If it is a boy you can call him Augustus.

April
Gus!

Julia
It's all right.
I plan to have lots of children.

April
I plan to search further.
Take advantage of the light.

Mrs Sparrow
Good luck.

April *goes*.

Mrs Sparrow
So it's your big day tomorrow?

Julia
I loved everyone today.
I fell in love with the people on the bus.
I took a glance up the High Street,
and I saw everyone,
purposeful with shopping
and loved them too.

Mrs Sparrow
I know the feeling.

Julia
I could forgive anyone tonight, I see there's no malice,
because I know what people want:
And it's just love and care, that's all.

Mrs Sparrow
Tell me about the wedding, is it all planned?

Julia
We start with the cake
and there are fireworks for afterwards.

Mrs Sparrow
Do you trust him? Nick.

Julia
You have to love people unconditionally.
Trust them even to let you down occasionally.
Tomorrow, I've dreamed of it for months.
Tonight, it's as if I could embrace the air itself.

Mrs Sparrow
I remember when you couldn't come out into these woods,
not for stepping on them.

Julia
I wish my brother would come back.

Mrs Sparrow
Ralph, is he not coming for tomorrow?

Julia
It's a long training course, and very strict.

Mrs Sparrow
I can't remember where he is.

Julia
Too far to travel for one day.

Mrs Sparrow
And Nick?

Julia
Out on his stag night.

Mrs Sparrow
It's years since there's been one here.

Julia
I thought I heard something in the bracken.
You've not seen anything.

Mrs Sparrow
It's the visitor season.
I watch them, items get stolen from the Post Office.

Julia
I wonder what it was I heard.

Ralph *jumps naked from a tree.*

Ralph
Me Ralph, you Julia!

Julia
Ralph? Ralph!
Where have you been?
Ralph.
What have you done to yourself?
Oh Ralph, this is terrible.
Thank God, you're here.

Mrs Sparrow
Who do you think you are?

Ralph
I'm the wild man of the woods!

Mrs Sparrow
Pagan!

Mrs Sparrow *goes.*

Julia
Ralph.
Where have you been?

Ralph
I have come through a green labyrinth.

Julia
What?

Ralph
Come with me.
I'll take you to the marshes,
we'll lie there at dawn,
naked under the water,
just eyes and nostrils above the surface.
You can feel the eels brush you,
frogs climb on you:
and when the sun rises
you'll see the steam over you.

Julia
No Ralph, I can't.

Ralph
Let's go now.

Julia
What is it, this green labyrinth?

Ralph
I've been travelling, all over, hundreds of miles and mostly at night. Often I've come to cities and turned from the yellow lights. Where I can I keep to the forestry, and only cross the open land in darkness. I've kept clear of the motorways, not following any path, except twice I came to the coast, I don't know which, and then I followed the shore for a while. I couldn't tell you which counties, woods, cities or seas I've seen. I determined to lose track; perhaps I crossed my own path sometimes, even doubled up part of the journey. It has been a green labyrinth. Come now, share it with me.

Julia
I can't Ralph, I'm getting married tomorrow.
Look this apple, it's a wedding present.

He takes it.

Don't eat it.

He eats it.

Ralph
You getting married?

Julia
Yes.

He snorts.

Julia
I hate not knowing where you are.
You could have stayed at home and signed on.
Where have you been?
I write you letters in my head.

Ralph
What do you expect, replies?

Julia
We've all lied for you, you know.

Ralph
I didn't ask anyone to cover up.

Julia
Why can't you do something for me?
Couldn't you just come to the wedding?

Ralph
Like this?

Julia
You'd need a bath.

Ralph
Why this sudden marriage interest?

Julia
Six months! The longest I've not seen you.
Everyone has to make their way in the world.
I'm twenty-nine, in less than twelve years I'll be over forty.

Ralph
Is he performing the service?
Our father in heaven.

Julia
Yes he is. They've been worried you know.
She blames him and they're not talking.
Can't you see why I want you there?
You've not even met my husband.

Ralph
What's he like?

Julia
Different.

Ralph
He'll need to be. Does he know anything about me?

Julia
No, nothing, what could I say?

Ralph
Would I like him?

Julia
He and you are the most important people to me now,
that's why I want you to meet.

Ralph
He and I, eh? He, and I.
Come with me Julia.

Julia
Stop it Ralph, let go of me.
Don't look at me.

I've thought of you for months, missed you!
but at this moment I wish you'd not come back.
It's as if you weren't my brother at all, it means nothing.

Ralph
I'll be off then.

Julia
Don't do that.

Ralph
Goodbye whoever you are,
have a happy marriage.

Julia
I don't understand, we've not talked yet.

Ralph
We've talked enough.

Julia
What do you eat?

Ralph
I take vegetables from the fields and I killed some sheep.
Cut them up with my knife.

Julia
What are you up to? When shall I see you?

Ralph
You won't, unless you come now.

Julia
Don't say that.

Ralph
You and I, we're tied, a blood tie, the only real tie.

He kisses her.

Julia
I do want to be with you.

Ralph
You have a choice.

Julia
You're giving me a choice?
I can't do what you do.
I don't want to escape, run away.

Ralph
I've never spent so many months on my own, it's no escape.

Julia
Tomorrow, that's really important to me.

Ralph
Brother or husband?
Husband or brother?

Julia
Doesn't it look as if I've chosen,
I shall go to my wedding tomorrow,
I'll be his wife, but still your sister.
It's not a choice.

Ralph
Except now.

He makes to go.

This is the end.

Julia
No!

Ralph (*he holds out his hand*)
This is the beginning?

Julia
No!

Ralph
What then?

Julia
Just part-way.

She runs off, he sits.

Nick *enters.*

Nick
Did I hear a voice?

Ralph
There was a woman here.

Nick
Oh I know who that was.

Ralph
Who are you?

Nick
Just a visitor.

Ralph
Where are you going?

Nick
I haven't decided.
Do you live here?

Ralph
No.

Nick
Me neither.
Where do you stay?

Ralph
I just lie down in the leaves at night.

Nick
That's what I'm always saying.
What do you do?

Ralph
Each night's supper provides every day's occupation.

Nick
Like everyone else.

Ralph
Can you take care of yourself?

Nick
Yes.

Ralph
Then do it, and try not to hurt anyone else.

Nick
I get these attacks of why?

Ralph
Why?

Nick
Yes.

Ralph
There's only doing and getting, keeping on.

Nick
Do you have a sense of humour?

Ralph
Hah! That was below the belt.

Nick
It's not a question with an answer?

Ralph
Why did I start talking to you?
No chat for months and now this.

Nick
It's an attractive game, running naked on a summer's night,
but in winter?

Ralph
I'll roll in the snow to warm my flesh
and by then my feet will be hardened sufficiently.

Nick
I don't believe you.
Why not make a fire?
Or build a house?

Ralph
You live with the cold.

Nick
And if it's like last year?

Ralph
Then you be careful not to stand on a rock
or it takes the skin off your foot.

Nick
You're disturbed, upset.

Ralph
I'm not a case.

Nick
Perhaps you act more strangely than you realise.

Ralph
Everyone's more self-deceiving than they know.

Nick
Can I come with you?

Ralph
This'd not be comfortable.

Nick
It must be killing you.

Ralph
I get to look at things as they are.

Nick
Do you think we are social creatures?

Ralph
Isn't it what sets us above the apes?
Collaboration.

Nick
Perhaps we made a mistake?
Contradictions abound!
First there's our relatives, we rarely get on with them.
As soon as we are old enough, we escape.

Secondly, we expect to choose others to live with and get on
with better than the relatives we had to live with.

And the result is spending your life doing what you don't
like, for reasons you don't comprehend.

Couples; it doesn't work.
Coupling; it doesn't interest me.

Ralph
So why do people do it?
Even my sister's getting married.

Nick
People feel incomplete.
No one wants to take care of themselves;
so they make a bargain:
you take care of me, I'll take care of you.
Taking care of you, I'm taking care of me;
and it becomes: my wife before you, my husband before you
and our children before everyone.
Horrible!

Ralph
But natural.

Nick
It doesn't make for a generous world.

Ralph
You expect a generous world?

Nick
I don't know.
But to do what you do, I see that as the best challenge.

Ralph *kisses* **Nick**. *He takes* **Ralph**'s *hand*.

Ralph
Into the night then.

Exit **Ralph** *and* **Nick**.

Enter **Julia** *from elsewhere*.

Julia
Ralph?

(*Aside*.) Gone.

Act Two

Late. **Julia** *and* **Mrs Sparrow** *talking.*

Julia
I had a bath.
I didn't recognise my body in the bath.
I knew something was going to happen.
I made tea. I poured tea into the milk jug.
I knew it would be like this.

Mrs Sparrow
Tomorrow, it will be all right.

Julia
Why should I let Ralph spoil my day?

Mrs Sparrow
Nothing will happen after all.

Julia
He wasn't going to come,
and now he isn't going to come.

Mrs Sparrow
Exactly. What's the difference?

Julia
My father will regret he ever let him go outward bound.

Mrs Sparrow
Your brother, he always was an outdoor man.

Julia
He misses Ralph.
He says he feels outnumbered, by women, two to one.
He puts the lavatory seat up. We put it down.
He says he's losing grip.

Mrs Sparrow
So Ralph's return would even things up?

Julia
No, my departure will do that.

Mrs Sparrow
Unless Stella finds him.

Julia
I don't hold out much hope.

Mrs Sparrow
Never dismiss the kindness of strangers, even tourists.

Julia
I went to Ralph's old room, earlier.
Nick stays there tonight.
I sat at the window, curtains open
and found I was waiting, hoping he'd come.

Mrs Sparrow
Why did you come out?

Julia
I felt alone and I got to thinking.
I didn't want to go to my single bed again.
I wanted the night to be over.

Mrs Sparrow
Will you sleep now?

Julia
I'd like to find Nick. Wake him, should I?
Does that shock you?

Mrs Sparrow
I understand.

Julia
I'd rather not be understood, no mystery then.

Mrs Sparrow
You lied to me earlier, about Ralph.

Julia
That wasn't a lie, it was a secret.

Mrs Sparrow
Is there a distinction?

Julia
Should I tell him?
Nick.

He has to know one day.
It's an uncomfortable secret.

Mrs Sparrow
Not tonight. Let it wait.

Julia
I am so incredibly angry what can I do?

Mrs Sparrow
Are you warm enough?

Julia
Quite warm enough, but tired.
I must make an effort to be my best.

Mrs Sparrow
Let me take you back.

They go.

Enter **Nick** *and* **Stella** *from opposite directions.* **Nick** *is dirty and has lost his jacket and tie.*

Stella
Julia sent me.

Nick
Ah!

Stella
You know who that is?

Nick
Yes.

Stella
Then you're the man I'm looking for.
She sent me to look for you.

Nick
What?

Stella
Now then: she wants you to come back for tomorrow.
She wants you to understand that even after the wedding there's no reason why you can't communicate. She says that she isn't at all ashamed of you and she asked me to emphasise that it's very important to her that you be there.

Nick (*aside*)
My head it's a gyroscope!

Stella
I just met her and I'm only doing this as a favour because she is so upset, but I think she will go ahead without you if necessary.

Nick
How?

Stella
What's happened to you?

Nick
I met this man in the woods, he was strange, he didn't have any shoes on; but he's gone now. He took me all over the place, and though we walked for hours, perhaps he led me in a circle, because I think I was here before.

Stella
Déjà vu perhaps?

Nick (*aside*)
Just when I decided to go back,
get the note back, now it's too late!

Stella
She cried.

Nick (*aside*)
And when you want a letter to get there it never does . . .

Stella
She was frantic.

Nick
Thank God I met you.

(*Aside.*) It's better to know . . .

Stella
She sat and brushed her lips on the back of her hand.

Nick (*aside*)
What if I had turned up after the note?
Horrible!

Stella
Only a madman would be out in these woods at night:
I've done my bit, goodbye.

Nick
Hey! Where are you off to? Can I come with you?

Ralph *enters with a lump of cake.*

Stella
Another one!

Ralph
Who wants cake?

Stella
Christmas cake in summer?

Ralph
Wedding cake!

Stella
Who's getting married?

Nick
Not me!

Stella
You stole this?

Ralph
Yes.

Nick (*aside*)
All my life is slipping away tonight . . .

Ralph
Look at the sky, it's like an aquarium or a deep swimming pool,
upside down.
And filled with stars.

Nick (*aside*)
I was on the brink and now I'm falling.

Stella
You don't think what you see is what's there do you?
How nostalgic can you get!

Nick
Everything slips through my hands . . .

Stella
So you're the strange man with no shoes on.
He told me.

Ralph
He asked to come with me.

Stella
He asked me that too.

Ralph *threatens* **Nick** *with his knife.*

Ralph
I could kill you and you wouldn't know it.

Nick (*to* **Ralph**)
You have such brown eyes.

Ralph (*to* **Nick**)
Cut your wrists with a blade of grass?

Stella
Is it possible?

Ralph
A reed would be easier.

Nick
I'm snatching at water!

Ralph
It's warmer at night. You can slip beneath the surface,
lean back, lie back, let yourself down into the black water.
Would you like that?

Stella
It's not dark here is it?
I've been walking in the half light.
I expected pitch darkness.

Ralph
It's only the lights over there that make it feel dark out here.

Nick
I don't agree! It's dark here.
I've never been anywhere so fucking black!

Ralph *slaps him.*

Stella
What's wrong with him?

Ralph
He's feeling incomplete.

Nick
The grass it's heaving,
as if the soil were breathing.

Stella
You never know what you might step on out here.

Ralph
With bare feet you know where you step.

Ralph *wrestles* **Nick**'*s shoes and socks from him.*

Nick
Why are you doing this to me?

Ralph
It only takes two months for the skin to harden.

Nick
How will I manage without my shoes?

Ralph
People managed before.

Nick
No. No. No!

Stella *assists* **Ralph** *in restraining* **Nick**.

Stella
Do you know him?

Ralph
No. Do you know him?

Stella
No.

Ralph
All strangers then.

Nick
My stomach it's churning.
Eels at the root of my gut!

Stella
Would cake cheer him up?

Nick
I'll not eat what's been on the ground.

Ralph
Everything's been on the ground.

Stella
He should eat some of that cake.

They struggle to force cake into **Nick***'s mouth.*

Nick
I'll not stomach this.

He goes.

Ralph
Do you want cake?

Stella
I don't like it.
Perhaps we could have been more sympathetic?

Ralph
He got what he deserved.

She looks. A point of light crosses the sky.

Stella
A shooting star.

Ralph
We know that was there.

Stella
It was there; or it was a plane.

Ralph
What about the moon?
We've been there, know about that.

Stella
The event of our lives; and it's forgotten.

Ralph
Dates have become titles for science fiction.

Time has been parcelled out.
The decades are so distinct,
I can't fit this century together.

Stella
We are the fools;
fools confined in a corner,
the scuffed corner of history,
a dog-ear of time.

Ralph
Such a monumental labour
to carve out the world
and we've left a great big hollow
with a little hard egg.

Stella
How long have we got?

Ralph
They may have lost thirty-two years somewhere,
and eleven days somewhere else,
but it's nearly done.
A crack between the clock's hands' clap! (*He claps.*)

Stella
Everyone thinks they're getting somewhere
and they're not.
I watch people running in the park
and I wonder, what are they running from?

Ralph
Perhaps they are only running?

Stella
Have you been Inside?

Ralph
No; outside for six months.

Stella
Do you have a Disease or something?

Ralph
No. I just eat irregularly.

Stella
Are you living on the dole too then?

Ralph
On my six wits.

Stella
If the world doesn't owe us a living
what do we owe the world?

Ralph
Why should we do anything?
It's late at night.
I like just to be somewhere like this.

Stella
How did you take to the wild life?

Ralph
I was here once.
Trees overwhelmed me.
I walked beneath them.
I went up to one, wrapped myself against it,
clasped the trunk in a great hug, gripped it between my legs,
the bark on my face.
Inside me, I had changes.
From then on, I came back often,
and walked here for miles,
naked at night.
So it became the only choice,
when events turned out as they did.

Stella
It must be odd out here,
quite different from getting undressed in a room.

Ralph
You put your clothes on a branch and walk away . . .

Stella
Don't ever try this in a park will you?
or you'll get arrested.

Ralph
What happened to you?

Stella
What do you do when you don't want to go home?
I walked on.

Ralph
Didn't you have friends?

Stella
You think you know someone and you don't.
You don't know anyone.
However many friends you have, it doesn't matter.

Ralph
But we hit it off instantly!

Stella
I don't have a scrap of self-pity.
I wouldn't have done this if it didn't thrill me.
It has been my most vivid year.
The most taste, the most smell, the most colours I've seen.

Ralph
Do you cry often?

Stella
No one talks you know.
People sit on transport,
faces knotted and don't speak.
I started a one-woman campaign:
spoke simply to provoke.
You should see how annoyed they get.

Ralph
But I like not-talking.

Stella
I want just to communicate.
They think you're after something.
It's the healthy ones interest me.
You especially.

Ralph
Me, healthy?

Stella
You are the most alive one I've met.

Ralph
Natural man meets strange woman!

Stella
For me it's been back to the wall
and for you it's been back to the woods.

Ralph
Let's not talk much now,
or we'll get bored with each other too quickly.
I like blackcurrants at night; after cake.
Shall we get some?

Stella
The world's out there.

Ralph
Believe me there's a world here.

Stella
Most of humanity I despise them.

Ralph
Me too!

Stella
Isn't it lucky I like you?

Ralph
It wasn't luck.

Stella
What else leads us where we go?

Ralph
Blackcurrants?

Stella
Let's go together then.

They go.

Nick *returns searching.*

Nick
They must be here somewhere.

April *enters.*

April
I am a tiger.

Nick
Where are my shoes?

April
Let's fight like tigers!

Nick
I'm looking for my shoes.

April
Leave it. Don't tell me. I like it:
the Unexplained.
Perhaps you walk on hot coals?

Nick
My life it only seems like that.

April
Aren't you going to ask about me?

Nick
No. I don't care.
Not out for a walk, that's certain.
People never are, there's always more to it than that.

April
It's true. I've come for the light.

Nick
Then you've come to the wrong place.

April
The light at dawn, at midsummer.
All sorts of things can be revealed.

Nick
I'm looking for a friend, a little bit of quiet and a true friend.

(*Aside.*) Why did he go off?

April
You can come with me.

Nick
No thanks.

April
Accept it then, there's no one else here.
You alone.

Nick
It's not true.
This place it's crawling with people.
Where I am,
I don't know if I should be here.
What I am doing,
I'm not sure if I should be doing it.
Perhaps I need a sign?

April
Fate, I believe in that.
Nothing is as random as you think.

Nick
Perhaps it's my destiny to be like this?

April
No. Unhappiness it's a vice.

Nick
I have such bad luck with people.

April
Everyone gets an even deal of luck.

Nick
How's that?

April
It's the inequality of chance.
A coin is as likely to fall heads as tails.
Yet after five hundred times heads,
it is no less likely to be tails next time.

Nick
Explain it.

April
You need to think of your own example.

Nick
Hmm! Can't think of any now.
I have to admit I am confused.

April
That's a good start.

Nick
Sometimes I wake in the night
I hear someone call my name;
and I half recognise the voice,
but I don't know who it is.

April
The Unexplained, we have to look at it rationally.
I can see you appreciate what I'm talking about.
Look at you, you're very untidy.

Nick
But this is just how I am tonight; you are too.

April
It's how things are.

Nick
What things?

April
These are the twin principles: the Untidy and the Unexplained.

Nick
It's a mystery to me.

April
You've got the picture.
Believe me, all over the world
people are thinking like this.
It's exciting isn't it?
Such a lot we'll never know.
Whole new fields opening up.

Nick
Fields with cows in them, that's all I know about.

April
Yes, but how do you know they're there?

Nick
Because the milk comes every morning.

April
It's a new era.
Doesn't it thrill you?

Nick
You are the most inconsistent person I've ever met.

April
I'm talking about a lot of old knowledge, dug up.

Nick
A lot of old ignorance you mean.
I may be blind but I'm walking in the dark.
I don't know where I'll get to, but I'm going.

He goes.

April (*aside*)
At least I know I'm lost.

She lies down in the leaves, clutching the stick.

I want to be covered.
I want to be pressed into the ground;
and I want to know nothing.

Julia *enters.*

Julia
Nick?
I'm looking for a husband.

April
You were the woman who wanted children.

Julia
Yes.

April
There was a man here with no shoes on.

Julia
Him. What did he say?

April
He was unhappy. He was looking for a friend.

Julia
Poor Ralph. Completely alone.
I shouldn't have left him.

April
It was someone particular, but not you.
He said it was a he.

Julia (*aside*)
Strange.

(*To* **April**.)
If you meet him again tell him I forgive him completely.
Say I beg him to come back.
I'll stick with him for life now.
How I wish Nick was here, he'd find Ralph.
How I need him now.
And to think I was full of guilt,
because of my impatience and anger.

April
Guilt it's not an admirable emotion.
But your impatience and anger,
they are virtues.

Julia
Where can Nick be?
I had a secret to tell him; it's a problem.
I'm frightened. What shall I do?

April
A secret is something you choose not to say.
But what about the things you don't know,
that you can't choose to say?

Julia
It's the things you don't know you know that frighten me.
You still have the stick, I see.

April
Every woman should carry a stick.
You never know what you might find.

Julia
First my brother ran away,
then my husband went missing
now I can't even find my father.
What's happened to all the men?
Why is everything suddenly in such chaos?
or is it my imagination?

April
It always has been
and now you've come to see it.

Julia
All these disasters,
storms, fires, crises,
sometimes I think I did them,
I hear the news and I think 'What have I done?'
That's stupid isn't it?

April
No. What fascinate me are the things
you don't know you don't know.

Julia
Oh, life's too short to worry about them.

April
Exactly.

Julia
So what's the answer?

April
They are all inside you anyway!

Julia
As I suspected, my fears are rootless.
I'll take one last look round and go home.

She goes.

April (*aside*)
It's too easy to dismiss what you can't explain.

Act Three

Early. **Mrs Sparrow** *and* **April** *talking.* **Mrs Sparrow** *has the note.*

Mrs Sparrow
There are two kinds of people in this world.
Those who go to the lavatory and those that don't.
That's my opinion.

April
Not everyone admits what they can do.

Mrs Sparrow
Mostly I'm concerned with the things I didn't do.

April
But you've obviously achieved such a lot:
the Post Office.
Think of all those millions of letters delivered.

Mrs Sparrow
Have you seen Julia?

April
She was looking for that man, the one with no shoes on.
She gave me a message. She said I was to say she begged
him to come back and to tell him she'd stick with him for life
if he did.

Mrs Sparrow
A family reconciliation might help things.

April
She said she wanted children.
She wants to marry him.

Mrs Sparrow
Who's this? Who? Did she mention his name?

April
Ralph, that's what she called him. I'm certain of it.

Mrs Sparrow
There are some things you'd rather not know aren't there?

April
Why need she marry him, just to have children?

Mrs Sparrow
Marriage, that's an obscene idea!

April
It's not for everyone.

Mrs Sparrow
Perhaps I should go now and tell the parents?

April
Why do people blame parents when it comes to sex?

Ralph and **Stella** *enter, heavily smeared with blackcurrant juice.*

Ralph
Because no one can imagine their parents doing it.

Mrs Sparrow
Where did you come from?

Ralph
I was under a blackcurrant bush.

Stella
That's a lie.

Ralph
Everyone doesn't speak truth.

Stella
That's a lie too.

Mrs Sparrow
I'd prefer it if it was so.

Stella
I found him.

Mrs Sparrow
I wish you'd not tried.
I wish you'd go away and not come back.

Stella
You're the ungrateful one.
Why is it people like you
always treat people like us,

like this?
No wonder he ran away.

April
Why this conflict,
is it the temperature?

Mrs Sparrow
I must say what I think.
This animal instinct,
you need to curb it.

Mrs Sparrow *goes.*

April
Are you a savage beast then?

Ralph
Everyone likes a good quarrel.

Stella
You have to recognise injustice.

April
There's no injustice.
All's for us to learn from.

Stella
And the holocaust, bombs, cancer?
They're not bad?

April
You don't understand.

Stella (*to* **Ralph**)
Why did she turn on me?

Ralph
Is it my fault?

April
Everything that happens you choose it.

Stella
What did I do wrong?

April
You create your own world entirely.

Ralph
Our parents, did we choose them?

Stella
Perhaps you'll learn something from this?

Stella *breaks* **April***'s stick.*

April
I reject your violence
because I have no doubt you have a right to feel alienated.

Ralph
Can't you allow us a bit of fun?
It's just an old stick.

April
I use it to find things beneath the soil.
There's always water moving underground.
I can feel it.

Stella
What nonsense!
How can you feel a thing like that?
I went to the biggest cemetery there is.
A hundred and eighty thousand dead,
beneath my feet,
and I felt nothing.

Ralph
Isn't there a machine you can get to do that,
detect things underground?

April
There's always a ghost in the device,
any machine inherits the quality of its maker.

Stella
Last time I bought a ticket
the machine spat it out.
The thing hit me in the chest
and fell on the floor.

Ralph
We used to have a microwave
until I put a hot water bottle in it.
Nothing works properly.

April
Back to nature,
is that the answer?
I'm attracted too.

Ralph
What exactly are you searching for tonight?

April
A man.

Stella
I've heard this before.

Ralph
I'm a man, perhaps it was me you wanted?

April
The one who was unhappy,
have you seen him?
Julia gave me a message.
She begs him to come back.
Do you know who that is?

Stella
You too.

Ralph
It all joins up now!

April
How much do you embrace?

Ralph
Everything! It's tangled up.

April
At last! What I've been searching for.

Stella
What's going on?

Ralph
This is chaos:
EVERYTHING'S ALL MIXED UP!

April
You have said it.

The pulse of nature,
I have felt it.
Now I go.
Thank you.

April *goes*.

Ralph
I think I begin to understand something.

Ralph *picks up the stick*.

Ugh!

Stella
What is it?

He throws it into the bushes.

Ralph
It twitched!
The stick twitched.

Stella
Are you all right?

Ralph
This is just life coursing through my veins,
but I don't know what that was.

Stella
The imagination can play tricks.

Ralph
Questions breed.

Stella
Where do questions get you?

Ralph
Sometimes I'm far from anywhere.

Stella
This life's untenable.
One day they'll find you
in a marsh somewhere

half-starved and dead of exposure.
Doesn't that frighten you?

Ralph
No.
What frightens me
is when a branch lashes unexpectedly
and you think there's something there.

Stella
What kind of thing?

Ralph
You know what I mean,
everyone's minds are similar in this respect:
A scaly pig-wolf thing
with serrated teeth and big claws.
It doesn't matter how educated you are,
it's still there crouching
horns pricked, eyes a-glitter, and wheezing smoke.

Stella
You are a curious lad.
Is that why you stay awake at night?
It's not the things of any other world that frighten me
but what people can do in this.
Just walking out here reminds me
of those bodies they find in the woods,
so decayed they have to remake the faces
even to guess who they were.
That's years ago now,
but I still can't go to the dentist
without feeling it's my face he's remodelling in clay
onto the skull bone.
Just the touch of these leaves
and I'm being laid beneath them,
seven years old and still clutching my satchel,
warm blood on the skin.

Ralph
All the soil is dead people.
Everything you eat is dead people.
Everything you drink passed through dead people first.

It's what we're made of:
we are dead people.

Stella
You should never say a thing like that,
because you never know what could happen.

Ralph
Then let's say all the dead people are living:
I got up from under the leaves and walked.
It also follows that we are everyone.
What everyone does we do.
What shall we do?

Stella
Let's go!

Ralph
How?

Stella
Get off. Get out. Go.
Why did anyone ever come here?
It was a mistake.
A bad idea to begin with.
This climate it's inhuman.

Ralph
Not inhuman, merely indifferent.

Stella
What's the earliest date you can remember?

Ralph
1066.

Stella
Less than a thousand years.
History's not begun here yet.

Ralph
But I found some Roman coins.

Stella
Brought from elsewhere . . .
This is not the ancient world.

Ralph
What about the early people who walked across the marshes
of the North Sea?

Stella
They began their journey somewhere else.
It's why people can't bear immigrants like me.
They only just stopped being immigrants themselves.
What's so special about this place?
The weather is a disaster.
It makes everyone miserable.

Ralph
Today was good. I lay in the sun for hours.

Stella
It's a big enough world.
Why spend your life in one corner?

Ralph
How do we travel over the water?
Now the Channel's not a marsh.

Stella
When I was eleven,
I climbed a runway fence,
got on a plane, ended up in Madrid.

Ralph
My sister has some plane tickets,
we could get them.

The branches lash, **Nick** *emerges, his clothes torn.*

Nick
Ralph, at last I've found you again!

Stella
Your feet, they're bleeding!
Don't cry.
Nick, your life is it all right?

Nick
I could cut up a sheep!
I can learn to swim!
You said you stole.

I do it too, in shops.
Only small things
but you should see how excited I get.

Ralph
You rub your face in the dirt don't you?

Nick
I'm a man of the soil now.
Ralph.
Please listen.
It means the earth.
Let me join you.

Ralph
You wouldn't last a minute out here.

Nick
It doesn't matter what you say.
I still want to do what you do.
My skin will harden too!

Nick *flings his shirt away. He begins to tear his trousers off.* **Ralph**
and **Stella** *go to stop him. They all grapple together.*

Stella (*to* **Nick**)
I saw him first!

Ralph
That's not so.

Julia *enters.*

Julia
You. You. And You!

Nick
Ah! Ah! Ah!

Julia
I went back and you weren't there.
I came out and you're back.
And you here, with them!

Ralph
He's with me.

Stella
I found him.

Nick
Hello.

Ralph
Do you two know each other?

Julia
He's my husband.

Stella
She's his brother.

Nick *and* **Ralph**
What?

Nick
Do you two know each other?

Ralph She's my sister. ⎤
Julia He's my brother. ⎦

Stella
What?

Nick
What?

Julia (*to* **Nick**)
What are you doing here?
You'd better wash your feet in the bath when we get home.

Stella ⎤
Ralph ⎦ He asked to come with me.

Ralph
You two do know each other!

Julia
Who do you think you are?

Ralph
A free man.

Julia
An outlaw!
What would happen if everyone thought like this?
Someone has to work.

Ralph
Don't work!
Millions can't be wrong.

Julia
Too many don't work, and they didn't choose.
The world doesn't run on its own.
Someone has to keep it going.
What gives you the right to behave like this?
Take what belongs to others?

Ralph
Not everything belongs to someone.

Julia
You are so green!
Everything I have, I have because I worked for it.
You have to work to achieve anything.

Ralph
Why work?

Julia
It's all we have to do. Most of us work to live.
We try to give our best in the service of others.

Ralph
Why should others want what you have to give?

Julia
I'd rather work than be unemployed.

Ralph
Then that's just vanity, and fear.

Julia
Fear and vanity?

She hits him.

Ralph
Yes.

Julia
What about self-esteem?

She licks her hand.

Blackcurrants!
All over your face.
There are no blackcurrants yet?
You've been home.
What have you done?
Don't you care about your mother and father?

Ralph
They are here.

Julia
No they're not, they're over there.

Ralph
They are in us.
We are them.
They are us. We are here.
I care, but I don't need to see them.

Julia
You are a selfish man.

Ralph
I am you.
You are me.
Meet you,
meeting me.

Julia
Don't make me think now.

(*Aside.*) I wanted to go to bed early.
I look forward to that, the moment I switch off.

Ralph
Listen to me. I am your redundant brother.

Julia
I'm not like you, Ralph.
I'm strange.
When it's raining I want to go indoors.
I like to read letters in the morning,
wash sweaters in the afternoon,
and cook supper in the evening.
When it's wet I prefer to be dry.
When it's cold I prefer to be warm.

None of this is as remarkable as you think.
It's what civilisation means.

Nick, shall we go home now?

Nick
No.

Julia
Why not?

Nick
I cannot do it.
I cannot give you that look.
You want a look of love.
I cannot give it.
I do not think I love you any more.

(And who's that?)

Julia
What about me?
I have it here.

Nick
If anyone is,
I am not for you.
Didn't you hear what I've been telling you?
(And why didn't you tell me about him?)
What did you expect?

Julia
Not this. Why now? Why not today?
What about tomorrow?

Nick
Today: it wasn't possible.
Tonight: it turned out this way.
and now Tomorrow: it won't happen.

Julia
You were the only person I ever chose.
You loved me?

Nick
I loved you.
I try to love you.

Julia
I don't want that. I want to be held by you.

Nick
I wish I could have loved you a bit longer.
(I wish you'd told me about him.)

Julia
The love of my life.
I had hopes.
You and I we could have had something.

Nick
We had it.
Don't be disappointed.

Julia
All my hopes have been destroyed,
how can I be disappointed?

Nick
You meet people once.
You love people once.
You lose people once.
So the next person you meet,
look them in the eye.

Julia
I want to get along.
Just let me get along.

Ralph
Here is a chance.

Julia
He took his chance.

Ralph
You have a chance.

Julia
He took my chance.

Ralph
We all have a chance,
but no one wants to look,
no one wants to think.

Julia
I prefer not to think.
I don't deserve this.

Ralph
You only have one chance.
And there you go, there you go,
throw away your only chance!

Julia
Was it you? or you?
What did you do to him?

Stella
You're not going to marry your brother are you?

Julia (*to* **Ralph**)
Did you take your chance with him?

Nick
It's no one's fault.

Julia
Everything in this world is someone's fault.

Nick
Don't take the responsibility on yourself.

Julia
It's not me I blame.

Nick
We have to tolerate each other,
we are all tolerated to some degree.

Julia
Ralph. How I dislike you.
I do not love you any more.
I hate you.
I could kill you.
Kill you and be quite happy.

Ralph
Except you haven't got it in you.

Julia
I could get your father's rabbit gun and shoot you down.

Stella
How can you say that to anyone?

Julia
He's my brother.
I can say what I like to him.
I'm allowed to hate him,
if I want to.

Ralph
We used to say that to each other when we were small.

Julia
I can see you have got together,
and it's been a plot,
a filthy plot.
It seems to me there's nothing left to say.

Stella
Take care of yourself.

Exit **Julia**.

Nick (*aside*)
She deceived me!
Why am I still here?
Why did I not go?
Hope can be a bad master.

Nick *retrieves his shirt*.

Stella
Did you love her?

Nick
I think I did.

Stella
If you love someone, you know it.
And if you don't, you don't.
She does.

Nick
I've been walking around with tears in my eyes for a month,
and she didn't notice, she was dreaming I think,
stars in hers.

Ralph
She had a lucky escape from you.

Nick
Thanks Ralph, can I have my shoes back now?

Ralph
I don't know where they are.
Haven't you more important things to consider?

Nick
It's not the same any more.
You've changed.

Ralph
You're a dog.

Nick
How?

Ralph
All men are dogs,
we have thighs like dogs.

Act Four

Not yet dawn. **Nick** *is urinating.* **Julia** *enters.*

Nick
Ah!

Julia
You.

Nick
I'm sorry.

Julia
I can take anything except apology.

Nick
I had to go somewhere.

Julia
Don't lick your finger.

Nick
It was wet, I didn't think.

Julia
Couldn't you have gone earlier?

Nick
I had to go now, it's how men are.

Julia
You could have gone back.

Nick
Too late.

Julia
Is it?

Nick
Julia.
If you ever need a hand, I am still your friend. Should you ever want any help I am still here, or would come if you called. If you ever wanted to come and find me, then do. If there's ever anything you need that I have, or could get for you, ask me.

As long as I am here I would support you.
I don't know why any of this is so,
except that your well-being is important to me.
And as far as I am concerned all this stands for always.

Julia
No one has ever hurt me as much as you did.
It became that I had no words
I could even share with you.
I could not speak.
Now I know that what you did is wrong,
but in spite of what you said I do not dislike you.

Nick
You loved me?

Julia
Yes.
You could not have been wholly aware of what you have done,
and so I wanted you to know that your act has had no effect
upon me, in case you should have regret.

Nick
Your face . . .

Julia
My face?

Nick
His face. I can see you have his face, it looks strange on you,
twisted and altered, and your hair it's different.
What can it be like to have a brother?

Julia
You'll never know.

Nick
Yes.

Julia
Sometimes you can drink coffee and think it tea.
Is that what happened here?

Nick
All I see now

is figures of people
before my eyes.

Julia
When you came near
I should have seen
you came by.

Nick
See you sometime then.

He kisses her.

Julia
I was askew,
but I do know what I do.

Nick *goes.*

Julia (*aside*)
He's gone,
run away,
from the wedding;
gone completely.
Who's going to cuddle me up now?
It's all I wanted
an hour ago,
and now?

Mrs Sparrow *enters.*

Julia
I never expected to be out all night.
I must look terrible.
My skin it's so flawed.
I hate it. I hate my skin.

Mrs Sparrow
You wear your doubts on your face.

Julia
Every time I look in the mirror,
it's the imperfections strike me first.

Mrs Sparrow
Better to have them on the outside,
where you can see them.

Julia
Is it?
Did you come to find me?

Mrs Sparrow
Yes.
The worst thing about this is that
you have lost solitude,
you can't bear to be alone.
But one day you will walk into an empty room and be thankful,
from then on you will be all right.

You and Ralph: let's not talk about it.
Has he gone back to the training course now?

Julia
Training, it's what they do to trees.

Mrs Sparrow
That boy needs training.

Julia
Ralph, he was born in a field with the gate open!

Mrs Sparrow
Forget about your brother. He's no good.
I am more concerned about you than him.

Julia
He is a pig.

Mrs Sparrow
A sister and a brother
shouldn't love each other.
I understand you. No mystery now.

Julia
Did you know we were twins?
Neither of us knows which is the twin.
We have been measured against each other,
measured ourselves against ourselves,
and we have both suffered.

Mrs Sparrow
Perhaps you should try to live with yourself?

Julia
How can you? When there's never you alone,
always you with the other.

Mrs Sparrow
Mostly there's just me.

Julia
Perhaps I will think differently,
when I get to your age.

Mrs Sparrow
At your age I was my age,
I think everyone always is.

Julia
I can see
I shall remember tonight
for the rest of my life.
These hours are etched in my mind.
I had this feeling earlier too, today.
Already it seems months ago,
now tonight has gone.

Mrs Sparrow
Did you sleep?

Julia
I was cold, I put the heater on,
I needed air,
I opened the window.

Mrs Sparrow
You had a little rest then?

Julia
I couldn't sleep for long
but I had a dream.
I was being force-fed eels,
a bucket of eels inside me.

Mrs Sparrow
What can have brought this on?

Julia
Do you think I shall have a child?

Mrs Sparrow
The best you can hope for is to sleep now.

Julia
I woke to find patterns in the room,
a sharp-edged print by moonlight,
squares on me.

Mrs Sparrow
So you're feeling better?

Julia
I'm not better,
I'm just acting.

Mrs Sparrow
What now?

Julia
I want a cake.
I'm going now to get a cake.

Mrs Sparrow
What for?

Julia
To eat. I must get one to eat, for my breakfast.
I'll go alone and eat my cake.
How did you know I might be here?

Mrs Sparrow
When you get to my age you know these things.

Julia
I hope I shall.

She goes.

Mrs Sparrow *takes out the letter.*

Mrs Sparrow (*aside*)
In spite of this gentle face,
I am an old square peg.
And though I may look soft
I have hard wooden corners.

Often I like myself very little
and it doesn't matter!
Sometimes it's better to say nothing.

She rips up the letter, then goes.

Nick *comes from where he has been concealed to gather the scraps of his letter.*

Nick (*aside*)
So it never got there.
That's the Post Office!
I could've gone back, but can't now.
It's too late,
and I don't want to
as I couldn't then.
What did Julia think?
Why did she say what she did?
It's a mystery – the unexplained.
Phew!
What an escape.

Ralph *and* **Stella** *enter.* **Ralph** *has a bag.*

Nick
I'm a free man now,
and I don't know what to do.

Stella
You've got a job.

Nick
A job is not what you do.

Ralph
You've got things.
Spend your money.

Nick
I've no money.
Just thirteen letters from the bank,
unopened.

Stella
Perhaps you'd like some cake now?

Nick
I'd like to try it.
See what it tastes like.

Ralph *breaks up a dirty lump of cake.*

Ralph
Brush the mud off first!

Nick
Woops.

Ralph
You don't want to get a tapeworm do you?

Stella
Who else will eat it?
Let's finish it.
We're off now.

Ralph
And our plans don't include you.

Nick
Good luck!

He showers them with the scraps of the letter.

Stella
How did you do that?

Nick
Magic!
Will I ever see you again?

Ralph
We'll go into 'phone boxes in dark lanes.
Try directory enquiries. We'll track you.

Nick
It could take forever.

Ralph
One of these old days we'll find you.

Stella
Arrive at night!

Ralph
Steal your shoes!

Stella
Wake you up with a bucket of water!

Nick
Perhaps I should go ex-directory?
I don't need this night-nettling nonsense.
How will you call?
You could use the Roman coins!
I eavesdropped earlier.

Ralph
We'll call reverse charges.

Nick *blows his nose.*

Nick
I think I have a summer cold.
I'd like that, to convalesce.
Stay in bed, eat beans.
Let friends take me for walks.

Stella
It's time you went and changed.

Nick
Everything I want to do.
When shall I do it?
It's going to be a race.
All this to do.
It fills me up.

Stella
You have your moments.

Nick
If I had a camera I'd take a picture.

Stella
Now you have a memory instead.

Ralph
I'll return, when you don't expect it.

Nick
I might live in expectation.
How will you know?

Ralph
I came here tonight, didn't I?
Though I didn't know a thing.
Who you were,
or what was happening.

Nick
Where could I ever find you again?

Ralph
Where the eels scutter,
Where the mud is warm,
Where the cress is thick,
Where the newts squirm,
That's where you'll find me.

Nick
Goodbye my friend.

He goes.

Stella
Why did you lie to him?

Ralph
I couldn't say where we were going.

Stella
But he knew about the Roman coins.

Ralph
You have to leave people in hope.

Stella
He knew you were lying.

Ralph
As I said it I meant it.
He knew that.

Stella
You are an outrageous forgetter.

Ralph
It's better to forget what you don't wish to know.

Stella
Is that Julia?

Ralph
What will she do now?

Stella
She'll find something.
A thing all of her own.

Ralph
How can I leave her?

Stella
Forget it. You'll never see her again.

Ralph
She's upset. I'm upset too.

Stella
Don't lose heart.
Wasn't it you who said 'Play your cards quickly'?
This is our only chance.

Ralph
How can we go on?
How will it end?

Stella
We've got our lives.

Ralph
I have nothing.
So I may as well risk everything.

Stella
I knew you were going to say that.

Ralph
We each know what the other is thinking.

Stella
We want to watch these conversations
or we'll get married to each other in our heads.

Ralph
My sister, she's like me, she needs sex
and she's not been getting any I expect.
That's always at the root of these problems.

Stella
So what have you been up to all these months?

Ralph
Let's not talk about that.

Stella
How much of what you've told me tonight is true?
You can be cruel, I see it.

Ralph
At least I don't pretend to be nice.

Stella
That wouldn't be easy for you.

Ralph
I flatter myself less than her.

Stella
But you are.

Ralph *smells* **Stella**.

Ralph
Did you take the scent?

Stella
No. I picked up a bottle in the dark
and it spilt, all over the wedding dress
but that wasn't scent it was ink.

Ralph
Then it's the smell of you that I like.

Stella
You're like the sun itself.

Ralph
How? Smiling and even-tempered?

Stella
No. In a constant state of explosion.

Ralph
Then you're the moon.

Stella
What? Changeable you mean.

Ralph
No. Powerful and there's more
than you chose to reveal.

Stella
Shall we revolve around each other then?

Ralph
Let's do it!

Stella
I'll not tell you any more about me.
No one's going to know what's in my head.
It's where I am.

Ralph
Are you inside there now, looking out at me?

Stella
Yes: I like you, you amuse me and I'm curious.

Ralph
We were made for each other?

Stella
Do we deserve each other?

Ralph
Shall we have the wedding now then?

Stella
Yes; in the church, before dawn.

Ralph
Not marriage?

Stella
No, just a wedding and then off for ever:
into the new millenium!

Ralph
What kind of ceremony?

Stella
I'll pass the gentle man an apple!

Ralph
I'll bring the lady acorns in cluster!

Stella
We won't promise anything.

Ralph
Make the preparations silent,
for the pagan wedding.

Stella
You plant branches flaming in the lawn.

Ralph
You fill the church with mistletoe.

Stella
I'll wrap my bike in ivy.

Ralph
Then fold back the flower bed,
this is the end of two thousand years!

Stella
Complete.

He takes a firework from his bag, sets it in the turf.

Ralph
I'll need a match.

Stella
I've found a match.

She goes to light the firework.

Ralph
Hey Stella, we wrote a book tonight!

Stella
We need a book for the journey.

She lights it.

Stella
Kiss me now.

They kiss, take one look and go.

Nick *enters and watches the firework, then* **April** *enters too.*

[*Unless it hasn't gone off, then:*

Nick
An unexploded firework:
let me try my new lighter.

If it now lights:

Nick
I always get emotional when
I see these things go off.

April *enters.*

If it doesn't light, then:

April *enters.*

Nick
This firework, it's not gone off.

April
I always expect things to go up at any moment,
and they never do!]

Nick
The pagans, they took my watch,
my beautiful gold watch,
it was a wedding present,
or perhaps I lost it.

April
They broke my stick too,
or I could help you find it.

Nick
There's enough sticks here.
I could break down a sapling.

April
No. I hate to see a tree come down.

Nick
They should chop this lot.
It would clear the view.

April
Tonight: I feel anyone could have taken my hand, kissed me;

and we could have gone together in the darkness; like animals.
You and I perhaps?

Nick
No. I've had enough: it's a decision.

April
Why are you still here then?

Nick
Don't you know what's been going on?

April
No one knows what goes on.

Nick
What are you doing?

April
Washing my face in the dew,
on Midsummer's morn.

Nick
Watch where you do that.

April
Nothing's cleaner than the dew.

Nick
Not any more it isn't.

April
We have to live with everything that's growing around us.
You can't discard anything.

She picks up the scraps of the letter.

It all stays with us.

She hands them to him.

There's no unfinished business.
Don't you have children?

Nick
Not that anyone's told of; yet!

April
Only a man can know that.

Nick
No. Not know? Yes.

April
There was a woman,
looking for someone.
Do you know her?

Nick
Yes. Know? No.

April
Did anyone call your name tonight?

Nick
Not a soul.
Nothing turns out as I hoped.
Why?

April
The unexpected; it keeps happening.
Why not just accept it all?

Nick
Because I hate it.
Because the news is always BAD!

April
Perhaps it should be a triple principle?
The Untidy, the Unexpected and the Unexplained?

Nick
I see most people as either
unhappy, unmarried or unemployed.

April
If I still had that stick I'd hit you with it.
As it is I give you this.

She takes out a clover leaf.

I shall live gleefully now
because I have had my moment of vision:
a naked man in the forest

like a revelation he appeared to me,
stepped from the trees and spoke.

She gives him the leaf.

Goodbye Ralph.

Nick
Who's Ralph?

He laughs.

April
You didn't expect to find yourself here did you?

Nick
I chose it.

April
The light will come soon, I know it.

April *goes.* **Nick** *eats the leaf.*

Nick (*aside*)
A long night for a short one.

He picks up the dead firework.

I think Julia will be fine.
Tenacious, that's her nature.
It's the one thing that's endless.

He pours out the dust, then reads the name.

'A Mine of Serpents.'

A loud ambiguous sound: a firework or a gun fired.

What was that?
It's early to be shooting.
Or was it whoever did this?

The sound again.

Have the pagans gone?

He listens.

It should be the low ebb of the night,
but in spite of that

I can hear the gods walking
and the years turning.

Mrs Sparrow *flies in.*

Mrs Sparrow
What can be louder than time?

It thunders.

Nick
How are you?

Mrs Sparrow
Oh, I've been dead for years.

He drops the firework.

Nick
What?

Mrs Sparrow
I've come to warn you.
The next thousand years . . .

Nick
Yes?

Mrs Sparrow
The next thousand years,
it will happen.

A lightning flash.

Nick
Oh no!
But I only wanted a better day today.

Mrs Sparrow
You don't deserve an inch,
so I give you a mile.

Nick
But if we have no end,
do we have anything?

Mrs Sparrow
Your answer, it's the question.

Nick
Two thousand years done,

and I have lived as if there was no tomorrow.
Now there is one.

Mrs Sparrow
And there's another thing: about tomorrow.

Nick
What's going to happen tomorrow?

Mrs Sparrow
Tomorrow you'll wake up
and find you're alive.
Then you'll be sorry.

She goes. It rains.

Nick (*aside*)
After tonight,
I'll not come back here,
not walk these woods again.
These feelings,
I leave them here,
tonight.
Let the ghosts walk
I'll not see them.

Today: I'll get through it.

Time to be gone
but I'll not walk now
I'll run,
and I'll be waiting
for that call.

(*To the audience.*)
If the world's too big to love one person what can you do?

Birds sing.

He throws the scraps of the letter high into the air.

The Modern Husband

A Play by Paul Godfrey
(1994)

After Henry Fielding
(1730)

'Honour the scenes which I presume
to lay before you with your Perusal.
As they are written on a Model I
never yet attempted, I am exceedingly
anxious least they should find less Mercy
from you than my lighter Productions.'
H.F. to P.G.

THE

MODERN HUSBAND.

A

COMEDY.

~~As it is Acted at the THEATRE-ROYAL in DRURY-LANE.~~

~~By His MAJESTY's Servants.~~

Written by ~~HENRY FIELDING, Esq;~~
Paul Godfrey

Hæc ego non credam Venusinâ digna Lucernâ?
Hæc ego non agitem? ————————
Cùm Leno accipiat Mœchi bona, si capiendi
Jus nullum Uxori, doctus spectare Lacunar,
Doctus & ad Calicem vigilanti stertere Naso.   Juv. Sat. 1.

LONDON:
Printed for J. WATTS at the Printing-Office in
Wild-Court near Lincoln's-Inn Fields.
————————
MDCCXXXII.   [Price 1s. 6d.]

For Nick

Characters

Mr Modern
Mrs Modern
Lord Richly
Mr Bellamant
Mrs Bellamant

The scene: London, 1730s.

The action occurs during the passage of one day and concludes the next morning.

The Bellamants are country gentry and the Moderns are a couple of urban parvenus.

Piquet and quadrille are related to whist.

This script was commissioned by the Actors Touring Company for a national tour directed by Nick Philippou and produced by Joanna Reid.

The **Moderns'** *parlour.* **Mr Modern**, **Mrs Modern** *at breakfast.*
Mr Modern *reads a summons.*

Mr Modern
Unless you can raise me five hundred pounds by tomorrow
night, I shall be in a fair way to go to jail the next morning.

Mrs Modern
If the whole happiness of my life depended on it,
I could not get the tenth part.

Mr Modern
Had you no success at cards last night?

Mrs Modern
Very indifferent.
I had won a considerable sum
if it had not been for that Lady Everplay,
she has such luck, if I were superstitious,
I should forswear playing with her;
for I never played with her but I cheated
nor ever played against her but I lost.

Mr Modern
Then without being very superstitious,
I think you may suspect that she cheats too.

Mrs Modern
Did I not know the other company –
for the very worst of the game of quadrille
is one cannot cheat without a partner.
The division of booty gives more pain
than the winning of it gives pleasure:
I have to make up accounts tomorrow with Mrs Sharpring
but where to get a hundred pounds I know not,
unless you have it, child.

Mr Modern
You do not manage Lord Richly right.
He is a person of considerable quality.
Men will give anything to a woman they are fond of.

Mrs Modern
But not to a woman whom they were fond of.

The decay of Lord Richly's passion is too apparent for you
not to have observed it.
He visits me seldom now.

Mr Modern
Then I see no reason for your acquaintance;
he dances no longer at my house if he will not pay the music.

Mrs Modern
I am afraid, should I ask a favour of him,
it might break off our acquaintance entirely.

Mr Modern
But hold, I have a scheme will oblige him to it,
and make better music than you imagine.

Mrs Modern
What is it?

Mr Modern
Suppose I procured witnesses of his familiarity with you
– I should recover swingeing damages.

Mrs Modern
But my reputation?

Mr Modern
Pooh, you will have enough to gild it;
never fear your reputation while you are rich –
for gold in this world covers as many sins
as charity in the next.
So that get a great deal and give away a little,
and you secure your happiness in both.
Besides, in this case all the scandal falls on the husband.

Mrs Modern
You will never persuade me:
my reputation is dearer than my life.

Mr Modern
Very strange! That a woman who made so little scruple of
sacrificing the substance of her virtue should make so much
of parting with the shadow of it.

Mrs Modern
'Tis the shadow only that is valuable:
Reputation is the soul of virtue.

Mr Modern
So far indeed that it survives long after the body is dead.
To me virtue appears nothing more than a sound
with reputation as its echo.
Is there not more charm in the chink of a thousand guineas
than in ten thousand praises?
But what need more argument:
as I have been content to wear horns for your pleasure
it is only reasonable you let me show 'em for my profit.

Mrs Modern
Husband, if my pleasures had been your only inducement,
you would have acted another part.
Sure, the wretch who sells his wife deserves another name?
How have you maintained your figure in the world
since your losses in the South Sea and elsewhere?
Do you upbraid me with crimes
which you yourself have licensed – have lived by?

Mr Modern
Had I followed my own inclinations, I'd have retired to the
country and reduced my pleasures to my fortune.
'Twas you madam who by your unbridled pride and vanity
ran me into debt and then I gave up your person to secure
my own.

Mrs Modern
Ha! Have I secured thy worthless person
at the expense of mine?
Did I not come unblemished to thee?
Was not my life as unspotted as my fame
till at thy base entreaties I gave up my innocence?
Oh! I had sooner seen thee starve in prison which yet I will
ere thou shalt reap the fruits of my misfortune.
No, I will publish thy dishonour to the world.

Mr Modern
Nay don't you do that.

Mrs Modern
Hypocrite!

Mr Modern
But child hearken to reason.

Mrs Modern
You call this reason?

Mr Modern
I admit myself in the wrong.
I ask ten thousand pardons.

Mrs Modern
Now I hear the voice of reason.

Mr Modern
. . . On this condition.
You obtain the money I require,
then I could forget the idea entirely.

Mrs Modern
I hear you. Now leave me a while that I may come to myself.

Mr Modern
My dear I am obedient.
Sure the grand seignior has no slave equal to a contented
cuckold.

Exit **Mr Modern**.

Mrs Modern *opens a letter*.

Mrs Modern (*aside*)
Tricksy's bill already!
What? Twenty pounds.
Bills! Bills!
I wonder in no civilised nation there is no law against 'em.
What shall I do?
Money must be raised but how?
Can I bear to be the public scorn
of all the malicious and ugly of my sex
or to retire to the country
with a man whom I hate and despise?
Is there on earth a person
that would lend me even twenty pounds?
Bellamant perhaps may do it:
he is generous and I believe he loves me.
Hold, there is a glimpse of hope that I may escape.
If his love is as violent as he swears it
now could I persuade him to fly away with me,

if he hath not too much tenderness for his wife.
I will write him this instant.
What wretched shifts are they obliged to make
who would support the appearance of a fortune
which they have not.

2

Lord Richly, **Mr Modern**.

Lord Richly
Mr Modern I am glad to see you here.

Mr Modern
My lord, I need to raise some money by tomorrow night
or I shall be in jail the next morning.
I would presume to remind your lordship of our agreement.

Lord Richly
You may depend upon it – I remember,
and I hope your lady is well.

Mr Modern
Entirely at your service my lord.

Lord Richly
Good. I have a particular affair to communicate to her:
a secret that I cannot send by you;
you know all secrets are not proper to trust a husband with.

Mr Modern
You do her too much honour my lord:
I believe you will find her at home any time today.

Lord Richly
Faith Modern, I know not whether thou art happier in thy
temper or in thy wife.

Mr Modern
My lord, as for my wife, I believe she is a virtuous woman,
that I think I may say of her.

Lord Richly
That thou mayest I dare swear; and that I as firmly believe
as thou dost thyself.

Mr Modern
My lord?

Lord Richly
Let me tell you a virtuous woman is no common jewel in this age.
But prithee has thou heard anything of Mr Bellamant's affairs?

Mr Modern
The disputed inheritance? No more than he lost his case –

Lord Richly
Undone, quite undone.

Mr Modern
– which he seemed to expect the other night,
when he was at my house.

Lord Richly
Then you are intimate?

Mr Modern
He visits my wife pretty often, my lord.

Lord Richly
Modern, you know I am your friend, let me warn you:
take care of Bellamant – he is prudent enough in his amours
to pass upon the world for a constant husband;
but I know him, he is a dangerous man.
Beware of Bellamant as you love your honour.

Mr Modern (*aside*)
Jack Bellamant may be of indifferent character.
But why should he warn me of him?

Lord Richly
I know you will excuse this freedom my friendship takes.

Mr Modern
Lord Richly, I am eternally obliged to you
so I hope your lordship will pardon my freedom
if I beg leave once more to remind you of my own necessity.

Lord Richly
Depend upon it, I'll take care of you.
My dear Modern, I am your most obedient humble servant.

(*Aside.*) What a poor chimerical devil is he?
Gaping for a favour
and without the least capacity of making a return.

Mr Modern
Thank you my lord.

Exit **Mr Modern**.

Lord Richly (*solas*)
Life may be properly called an Art
as any other,
the great incidents in it
are no more to be considered as mere accidents
than the several verses of a fine poem
or the scenes of a noble play.
As histories of this kind
may be properly called models of Human Life,
so by observing the several incidents
which tend to the catastrophe
or completion of the whole,
and the causes whence those incidents are produced,
we shall best be instructed
in this most useful of all arts
which I call the Art of Life.

3

The **Bellamants'** *house*. **Mr Bellamant** *reading a letter*. **Mrs Bellamant** *enters*.

Mr Bellamant
So soon returned my dear?

Mrs Bellamant
I have been in such an assembly of company and so pulled to pieces with impertinence and ill-nature. I shall welcome the country for sure the world is so very bad those places are best where one has least of it.

Mr Bellamant
What's the matter?

Mrs Bellamant
A surfeit of the town.
I have been downright affronted.
After all the nonsense and ill-nature I have heard today who
would grieve to part with the place where one is sure to hear
'em over again?

Mr Bellamant
Who durst affront you?

Mrs Bellamant
A set of women that dare do everything
but what they should do.
In the first place I was complimented with prudery
for not being at the last masquerade
– with dullness for not entering into the taste of the town
in some of its diversions;
then had my whole dress run over and disliked;
and to finish all Mrs Termagant told me I looked frightful.

Mr Bellamant
Not all the paint in Italy can give her half your beauty.

Mrs Bellamant
You are certainly the most amenable man in the world
and I the only wife who can retire home to be put in a good
humour.

Bellamant *folds the letter.*

Mrs Bellamant
Any woman who has with her in the country
the man she loves
must be a very ridiculous creature to pine after the town
and yet there are such creatures.
I imagine they retire with the man they should love
rather than him they do;
for a heart that is passionately fond of pleasures here
has rarely room for any other affection.
Yet the town itself is the passion
of the greater part of our sex
but such I can never allow a just notion of love to.
A woman who sincerely loves
can know no happiness without,

nor no misery with her beloved object.

Bellamant *puts the letter in his pocket.*

Mrs Bellamant
You seem discomposed my dear,
I wish there be no ill news in that letter?

Mr Bellamant
My dear I have a favour to ask of you.

Mrs Bellamant
Say to command me.

Mr Bellamant
I gave you a banknote of a hundred pounds yesterday.
You must let me have it again.

Mrs Bellamant
I am the luckiest creature in the world
that I did not pay away some of it this morning.

Mr Bellamant (*aside*)
Excellent! Unhappy woman!
How little doth she guess she fetches this money for a rival?
That is the little merit I can boast towards her:
to have contended
by the utmost compliance with all her desires,
and the utmost caution in the management of my amour,
to disguise from her a secret that would make her miserable.
Let me read once more.

'Sir – If you have any value for me
send me a hundred pounds this morning,
or to make 'em more welcome
than the last of necessities can be,
bring them yourself.
Yours more than her own,
HILLARIA MODERN'

Why, what a farce is human life!
How ridiculous is the pursuit of our desires
when the enjoyment of them is sure to beget new ones!

Mrs Bellamant
Here is the bill my dear.

They kiss. The letter falls from **Mr Bellamant***'s pocket.*

Mr Bellamant *exits.*

Mrs Bellamant
He will not speak of his losses.
The angel seeks to spare me all.
Yet I could not avoid noticing
how he put that letter from my sight.
Surely it must be bad news.
How lonely he must be in his hour of grief.
My heart is wrung out with pity
but I cannot share his burden
since I know nothing of his trials.

She sees the letter.

What's this? A bill? A demand for money?
There is more ill news, no doubt, in here.
It is my Christian duty as his wife
to read this letter
and thereby I may endeavour
to support my husband in his misfortune.

Mrs Bellamant *exits.*

4

Lord Richly, **Mr Bellamant**.

Lord Richly
Dear Bellamant, I am your most obedient servant.
I am come to ask you ten thousand pardons
that my affairs prevented my attendance
the day your case came before the Lords.
I am sorry I was not there.
It might have been in my power
to have served you beyond my single vote.
It went against you I hear.

Mr Bellamant
I am obliged to your lordship
but as I have reason to be satisfied
with the justice of the House, I am content.

Lord Richly
I hope the loss was not considerable.

Mr Bellamant
I thought your lordship had heard.

Lord Richly
I was told twenty thousand pounds
but that's a trifle, a small retrenchment in one's expenses,
two or three dozen less suits
and two or three dozen fewer women in the year . . .

Mr Bellamant
My loss is not equal to what your lordship intimates;
nor can I complain of a fortune still large enough to retire
into the country with.

Lord Richly
Nay, we must not lose you so.
Have you no friend that could favour you
with some snug employment
of a thousand or fifteen hundred per annum?

Mr Bellamant
Who?

Lord Richly
I am sure no mortal would do half so much to serve you as
myself but I can't help saying that these things are not easily
obtained.
I heartily wish that I could serve you in any thing.
It gives me a great deal of uneasiness that my power is not
equal to my desire.

Mr Bellamant
Then I am obliged to the good offices of my friend
but I assure you I have lived long enough in the world
to see that necessity is a bad recommendation
to favours of that kind,
which as seldom fall to those who really want them
as to those who really deserve them.

Lord Richly
Upon my soul Mrs Bellamant's a fine woman,
are you resolved to make her suffer your misfortune?

Would it not be civil to give her the choice?
A parliament man should always bring his wife to town
that if he does not serve his public she may.
There is a trade known to our ancestors
which unlike the modern bubble
seems to be in a rising condition at present.

Mr Bellamant
Ay, it is a stockjobbing age,
everything has its price;
even marriage is a traffic throughout;
as most of us bargain to be husbands
so some of us bargain to be cuckolds
and he would be as much laughed at
who preferred his love to his interest at this end of the town,
as he who preferred his honesty to his interest at the other.

Lord Richly
You Bellamant have had boldness enough
in contradiction to this general opinion
to choose a woman for her sense and virtue.
You must be the happiest man in the world to possess a wife
whom the sum of ten thousand pounds would have no effect
on?

Mr Bellamant
I look upon myself equally happy in having no friend who
would tempt her.

Lord Richly
That thou has not, I dare swear, but I thank you for putting
me in mind of it.

Mr Bellamant
As our stay will be so short in town
she can do you no service my lord
and besides I have heard her detest partiality in those affairs.
You would never persuade her to give a vote contrary to her
opinion.

Lord Richly
Detest partiality! Ha!
I have heard a lady declare approval of a play
and then condemn it the next minute

though she had neither seen nor read it.
These things are guided entirely by favour.

Mr Bellamant
Nay, I see no reason to fix the scandal on the ladies:
party and prejudice have the same dominion over us.
Ask a man's character of one of his party
and you shall hear he is one of the worthiest fellows in
Christendom;
ask it of one of the opposite party
and you shall find him as good-for-nothing a dog as ever was
hanged.
So that a man must labour very hard to get a general good
reputation
or a general bad one.

Lord Richly
And you, my dear Bellamant, have laboured very hard
and got nothing at all.
Is it true that you lost everything?

Mr Bellamant
That I allow at this moment
but I have hopes of overcoming the present calamity.
Maybe I am searching even now
for the means to retrieve the money?

Lord Richly
Well, since you allow so much
you will give me leave to tempt Mrs Bellamant.

Mr Bellamant
With all my heart, my lord.
She will be at home this afternoon.

Lord Richly
Thou art a well-bred husband indeed,
to give another leave to tempt your wife.

Mr Bellamant
I should have been a very ill-bred one to have denied it.

Lord Richly (*aside*)
If I had said more he had granted it
rather than lose my favour.
Poverty makes as many cuckolds as thieves.

5

The **Moderns'** *house.* **Lord Richly**, **Mrs Modern**. **Mrs Modern** *reading a letter, taking a hundred-pound note from the envelope.*

Mrs Modern
Ha! It is Bellamant's hand and the note that I desired.
This is lucky indeed.

Lord Richly *enters.*

Mrs Modern
I ought to blame your unkindness –
I have not seen you so long.

Lord Richly
Do you think a week so long?

Mrs Modern
Once you would have thought so.

Lord Richly
Why truly, hours in the spring of love are something shorter
than they are in the winter

Mrs Modern
Barbarous man!
Do you insult me after what I have done for you?

Lord Richly
I fancy those favours have been reciprocal.

Mrs Modern
Have I not given you up my virtue?

Lord Richly
And have I not paid for your virtue, madam?
I am fifteen hundred pounds out of pocket
which in my opinion is fourteen more
than any woman's virtue is worth;
in short our amour is at an end
for I am in pursuit of another mistress.

Mrs Modern
Why do you come to torment me with her?

Lord Richly
Why, I would have you act like other women
in a lower situation:
when you can please no longer with your own person,
e'en do it with other people's.

Mrs Modern
You monster! This is insupportable.

Lord Richly
Madam you may rave
but if you will not do me a favour there are people who will.
I fixed on you out of a particular regard to you
for I think when a man is to lay out his money
he is always to do it among his friends.

Mrs Modern (*going*)
I'll bear it no longer . . .

Lord Richly (*going*)
Nor I.

Mrs Modern
Stay my lord can you be so cruel?

Lord Richly (*going*)
Pshaw!

Mrs Modern
Oh stay! Stay! You know of my necessities.

Lord Richly
And I propose a very good cure for them.

Takes out his wallet.

Mrs Modern
Lend me a hundred guineas then.

Lord Richly
I will do more –

Mrs Modern
Generous creature!

Lord Richly
I'll give you twenty.

Mrs Modern
Do you jest with my necessity?

He gives her a twenty-pound note.

Lord Richly
Why should we use more decency to an old acquaintance
than you ladies do to a new lover,
and have more reason for so doing?
You often belie your hearts when you use us ill,
in using you so we but follow the dictates of our natures.

Mrs Modern
If you please my lord, why not truce with your proposals
and let piquet be the word?

Lord Richly
I know of none whom I would sooner lose to than yourself.
For to anyone who loves to play as well as you
and plays as ill,
the money I lose by a surprising ill-fortune is only lent.

Lord Richly *deals the cards.*

Mrs Modern
Methinks my lord you should be fearful of deterring me by
this plain dealing.

Lord Richly
I am better acquainted with your sex.
It is impossible to persuade a woman that she plays ill
as that she looks ill.
(*Aside.*)
She is one of those whose winning nobody ever heard of
or whose losing no one ever saw.

They play piquet. **Mrs Modern** *lays down the twenty-pound note
and the hundred-pound note as bets.*

6

Mr Modern
I am poured out like water
and all my bones are out of joint.

How quickly the hours fly away
while I am brought to the very threshold
of the prison yard.
Lord Richly is indifferent to my fate.
So why should I not extort all I can?
As for my wife,
why shouldn't she sacrifice her vanity
to buy a husband's freedom?
I grow impatient.
Sure, the bottomless pit awaits me
and already the morning is gone.
Unless she can raise the money
from one of her gallants
in these next hours
then I know what course I must take.

7

As 5, **Lord Richly** *and* **Mrs Modern** *at piquet.* **Richly** *wins the game.*

Lord Richly
I win.

Mrs Modern
Can you be so cruel?

Lord Richly
Ridiculous!
You might as well ask me for my whole estate;
I am sure I would as soon give it you.

Mrs Modern
An everlasting curse attends the cards!
To be repiqued from forty when I played but for five!
My lord I believe you a cheat.

Lord Richly
At your service madam,
when you have more money
if you will honour me with notice
I shall be ready to receive it.

He takes up the money.

Mrs Modern
Stay my lord, at least give me the twenty-pound note.

Lord Richly
On my conditions.

Mrs Modern
On any conditions.

Lord Richly
Lookye madam if you will do a good-natured thing for me
I will oblige you in return as I promised you before
and I think that very good payment.

Mrs Modern
Pray my lord use me with decency at least.

Lord Richly
Then you must contrive, by some way or other, a meeting
between me and Mrs Bellamant at your house tonight.

Mrs Modern
Mrs Bellamant!

Lord Richly
Why do you start at that name?

Mrs Modern
She has the reputation of the strictest virtue of any woman in
the town.

Lord Richly
Virtue! Ha!
So have you and so have several others of my acquaintance.
There are as few women
who have not the reputation of virtue
as have the thing itself.

Mrs Modern
And what do you propose by meeting her here?

Lord Richly
I am too civil to tell you plainly what I propose
though by your question one would imagine you expected it.

Mrs Modern
I expect anything from you rather than civility my lord.

Lord Richly
Madam, it will be your own fault if I am not civil to you.
Do this for me and I'll deny you nothing.

He gives her the twenty-pound note again.

Mrs Modern
There is one thing that tempts me more than your gold
which is the expectation of seeing you desert her,
as you have done me.

Lord Richly
Which is a pleasure you'll certainly have;
and the sooner you compass my wishes
the sooner you may triumph in your own.
Nay, there is a third motive will charm thee,
my dear Hillaria,
more than the other two.
When I have laid this passion
which hath abated that for you,
I may return to your arms with all my former fondness.

Mrs Modern
Excuse my incredulity my lord,
for though love can change its object
it can never return to the same again.

Lord Richly
I may convince you of the contrary.
But to our business:
Fortune has declared on our side already by sending
Bellamant hither.
Cultivate your acquaintance with him
and you cannot avoid being acquainted with his wife.
She is the perfect shadow of her husband,
they are as inseparable as Lady Coquette and her lapdog.

Mrs Modern
Or as her ladyship and her impertinence?
Or her lapdog and his smell?
It is to me surprising how women of fashion
can carry husbands, children and lapdogs about with them,
three things I never could be fond of.

Lord Richly
If the ladies were not fonder of their lapdogs
than of their husbands
we should have no more dogs in St James' parish
than there are lions at the Tower.

Mrs Modern
It is an uncommon bravery in you to single out a woman
who is reputed to be the fondest of her husband.

Lord Richly
She that is fond of one man may be fond of another.
Fondness in a woman, like the love of play,
may prefer one man and one game
but will incline her to try more;
especially when she expects greater profit –
and there I know I am superior to my rival.
If flattery will allure her or riches tempt her,
she shall be mine;
and those are the two great gates
by which the devil enters the heart of womankind.

Mrs Modern
You will have your opportunity at my house
and to procure it I must be acquainted with Mrs Bellamant.
Now is it not a lucky accident that Mr Bellamant is an
humble servant of mine?

Lord Richly
That is lucky indeed.
Could we not give her a cause of suspicion that way
it were a lively prospect of my success
– just as persuading a thief that his companion is false
is the surest way to make him so.

Mrs Modern
A pretty comparison of your lordship's between the two
states.

Lord Richly
Thou dear creature, let me but succeed in this affair
I'll give thee millions.

Mrs Modern
More gold and fewer promises my lord.

Lord Richly
A hundred guineas shall be the price of our first interview.

Mrs Modern
Be punctual and be confident.

Lord Richly
Adieu my Machiavil.

Lord Richly *exits*.

8

At the **Moderns'** *house, later*. **Mrs Modern**, **Mr Bellamant**.

Mrs Modern
Is it not barbarous, nay, mean, to upbraid me
with what nothing but the last necessity could make me ask
of you?

Mr Bellamant
You wrong me, I lament my own necessities,
not upbraid yours.
My misfortune is too public
for you not to be acquainted with it
and what restrains me from supporting the pleasures
of the best wife in the world
may, I think, justly excuse me
from supporting those of a mistress.

Mrs Modern
Do you insult me with your wife's virtue?
You! Who have robbed me of mine?
Yet Heaven will, I hope, forgive me this first slip;
I repent the day I heard the Siren persuasions
of your ungrateful sex.

Mr Bellamant
If I alone have robbed you of your honour,
it is you alone have robbed me of mine.

Mrs Modern
Your honour! Ridiculous! The virtue of a man!

Mr Bellamant
Madam I say my honour,
if to rob a woman who brought me beauty,
fortune, love and virtue;
if to hazard making her miserable be no breach of honour,
robbers and murderers may be honourable men:
yet this I have done and this I do still for you.

Mrs Modern
We will not enter into a detail Mr Bellamant
of what we have done for one another;
perhaps the balance may be on your side:
if so it must be still greater
for I have one request which I must not be denied.

Mr Bellamant
You know if it be in my power to grant
it is not in my power to deny you.

Mrs Modern
Then for the sake of my reputation
and to prevent any jealousy in my husband,
bring me acquainted with Mrs Bellamant.

Mr Bellamant
Ha!

Mrs Modern
By which means we shall have more frequent opportunities
together.

Mr Bellamant
Of what use your acquaintance can be I know not.

Mrs Modern
Do you scruple it?
This is too plain an evidence of your contempt of me;
you will not introduce a woman of stained virtue to your
wife:
can you who caused my crime be the first to condemn me for
it?

Mr Bellamant
Since you impute my caution to so wrong a cause
I am willing to prove your error.

Mrs Modern
Let our acquaintance begin this night then,
try if you cannot bring her hither now.

Mr Bellamant
I will try, nay, and I will succeed:
for oh! I have sacrificed the best of wives to your love.

Mrs Modern
I envy, not admire her for an affection
which any woman might preserve in you.

Mr Bellamant
I fly to execute your commands.

Mrs Modern
I must ask one last favour of you –
and yet I know not how –
though it be a trifle, and I will repay it –
only lend me another hundred pounds.

Mr Bellamant
Your request madam is always a command.
I shall think time flies with wings of lead till I return.

9

The **Bellamants**' *house.* **Mrs Bellamant** *with the letter.*

Mrs Bellamant (*solas*)
So he deceives me with another woman:
What choice have I but to forgive
that which is so commonplace,
it is perhaps the general mode of masculine behaviour?
He is kind. He treats me well.
The worst is that I love him.
That is what cuts me.
But is there any yoked creature
without its private opinion?
Though I ne'er before held any secret
now I feel licensed by his deception of me.
Thus I will conceal this letter
and not confront him with its contents

but instead seek to discover them together,
as if by chance.
And when the plain truth is apparent
then he may answer for it.
I must be patient
till Fortune delivers the opportunity.
Oh my husband!
It is for love of you
that I now trace your footstep
on the path of lies.

Enter **Lord Richly**.

Lord Richly
Mrs Bellamant you are a perfect deserter from the beau
monde.
It is the word of the town that you are an advocate against
play.

Mrs Bellamant
I am only for indulging reason in our entertainments my
lord.
I never intend to sacrifice my time entirely to play
until I can get no one to keep me company for nothing.

Lord Richly
Then I am here to be your servant,
shall I not have the honour of entertaining you at piquet?

Mrs Bellamant
Your lordship has such a vast advantage over me.

Lord Richly
None in the least,
but if you think so madam,
I'll give you what points you please.

Mrs Bellamant
For one party then my lord.

Lord Richly (*aside*)
Charming woman!
And thou art mine as surely as I wish thee.
Let me see, she goes into the country in a fortnight,
now if I compass my affair in a day or two
I shall be weary of her by that time;

and her journey will be the most agreeable thing that can
happen.

They play piquet.

10

Mr Bellamant (*solas*)
Why should I not enjoy a wife and mistress?
We are come to an age
wherein a woman may live very comfortably
without a reputation.
Why should I not do as other men?
I am mistaken if many husbands in this town
do not live very easily
by being content in their cuckoldry,
nay, by being promoters of it.
Marriage has presented the solution to my current
misfortune
in the form of a beautiful wife.
Dare I to hope she could be debauched?
It is a wonder to me that she doth not suspect my own
infidelity.
Why should I not present her with a liberty
that I myself enjoy?
Richly is a voluptuous fellow.
He oftener injures women in their reputation
than in their person.
Can she not send him away if she chooses?

11

As 9, **Lord Richly**, **Mrs Bellamant** *at piquet.*

Lord Richly
Six parties successively!
Sure Fortune will change soon or I shall believe she is not
blind.

Mrs Bellamant
No my lord, you either play with too great negligence

or with such ill-luck
that I shall press my victory no further at present.
Besides I can't help thinking five points place the odds on
my side.

Lord Richly
Can you change this note madam?

He produces the hundred-pound note.

Mrs Bellamant
Let it alone my lord.

Lord Richly
Excuse me if I am superstitiously observant
to pay my losings
before I rise from the table.
Besides madam, it will give me an infinite pleasure
to have the finest woman in the world in my debt.
Do but keep it till I have the honour of seeing you again.
Nay madam, I must insist on it,
I am forced to leave it in your hands thus –

Lord Richly *gives her the hundred-pound note and exits.*

Mrs Bellamant (*aside*)
What can this mean?
I am confident that he lost the last party designedly.
I observed him fix his eyes steadfastly on mine
and sigh and seem careless of his game
– it must be so – he certainly hath a design on me.
Here is the chance to revenge my husband
if I should desire it.

Enter **Mr Bellamant**.

Mrs Bellamant
My dear! Where have you been all day?
I have not had one moment of your company since breakfast.

Mr Bellamant
I have been upon business of great consequence my dear.

Mrs Bellamant
Is it fit for me to hear?

Mr Bellamant
No my dear it would only make you uneasy.

Mrs Bellamant
Nay then I must hear it that I may share your concern.

Mr Bellamant
Indeed it would rather aggravate it
for it is not in your power to assist me,
but since you will know it, an affair hath happened
which makes it necessary for me to pay a hundred pounds
this very evening.

Mrs Bellamant
Is that all?

Mr Bellamant
That indeed was once a trifle but now it makes me uneasy.

Mrs Bellamant
So it doth not me because it is in my power to supply you –
here is a note of that sum.

She gives him the same hundred-pound note again.

(Aside.) I know who this is for!
(*To* **Mr Bellamant**.) But I must be positively repaid within a
day or two:
it is only a friend's money trusted into my hands.

Mr Bellamant
My dear, sure when Heaven gave me thee
it gave me a cure for every malady of the mind
and made thee the instrument of all its good to me.

Mrs Bellamant
Be assured I desire no greater blessing
than the continual reflection of having pleased you.

Mr Bellamant
Are you engaged, my love, this evening?

Mrs Bellamant
Whatever engagement I have is in your power to break.

Mr Bellamant
If you have none I will introduce you to a new acquaintance:

one who I believe you never visited but must know by sight –
Mrs Modern.

Mrs Bellamant (*aside*)
La!

(*To* **Mr Bellamant**.) Husband, it is equal to me in what
company I am when with you.
My eyes are so delighted with that principal figure
that I have no leisure to contemplate the rest of the piece.

Mr Bellamant (*aside*)
What a wretch am I!
Have I either honour or gratitude
and can I injure such a woman?
Do I injure her?
While she perceives no abatement in my outward passion
she is not injured by its inward decay:
nor can I give her a secret pain
while she hath no suspicion of my secret pleasures.
Have I not found an equal return of passion in my mistress?
Does she not sacrifice more for me than a wife can?
The gallant is indebted for the favours he receives:
while the husband pays dearly for what he enjoys.
But I hope this will be the last I shall be asked to lend.
My wife's having this dear note was as lucky as it was
unexpected.
Ha! The same one I gave this morning to Mrs Modern.
Amazement! What can this mean?

(*To* **Mrs Bellamant**.) My dear be not angry at my curiosity,
but pray tell me how came you by this?

Mrs Bellamant (*aside*)
Should I reveal him the truth?
Who can tell into what suspicions it may betray him?
How nearly have I come unawares to the brink of disaster!
For surely the lightest suspicion of a husband is ruin indeed!

(*To* **Mr Bellamant**.) Pardon me my dear,
I have a particular reason for not telling you.

Mr Bellamant
And I have a particular reason for asking it.

Mrs Bellamant
I beg you not to press me:
perhaps you will oblige me to sacrifice a friend's reputation.

Mr Bellamant
The secret shall rest in my bosom, I assure you.

Mrs Bellamant
But suppose I should have promised not to suffer it from my
own.

Mr Bellamant
A husband's command breaks any promise.

Mrs Bellamant
I am surprised to see you so solicitous about a trifle.

Mr Bellamant
I am rather surprised to find you so tenacious of one;
be assured you cannot have half the reason to suppress the
discovery as I to insist upon it.

Mrs Bellamant
What is your reason?

Mr Bellamant
The very difficulty you make in telling it.

Mrs Bellamant
Your curiosity shall be satisfied then;
but I beg you would defer it now,
that I may get absolved from my promise of secrecy.
I beg you would not urge me break my trust.

Mr Bellamant (*aside*)
She certainly hath not discovered my falsehood,
that were impossible:
besides I may satisfy myself immediately by Mrs Modern.

Mrs Bellamant
What makes you uneasy?
I assure you there is nothing in this worth your knowing.

Mr Bellamant
I believe it, at least I shall give up my curiosity to your
desire.

Mrs Bellamant
I am ready to wait on you.

Mr Bellamant
I must make a short visit first on what I told you
and will call on you immediately.

Exit **Mr Bellamant**.

Mrs Bellamant (*solas*)
The world is grown strange to me.
I never deceived anyone in my life
and now I have become a seasoned liar
within the space of one hour.
Scruples melt like wax in the heat of circumstance.
Why does he want me to meet Mrs Modern?
Do they mean to insult me openly tonight?
I could not refuse without admitting what I have discovered.
I shall not flinch to face
something I hate and blush to see or hear.
And the banknote:
What can have given him the curiosity I know not.
If I had told him where I came by it
his jealous honour might have resolved
some fatal return to Lord Richly,
had he taken it the same way I do.
Whereas by keeping the secret
I preserve my husband every way from danger;
for I myself will secure his honour
without exposing his person.
I will personally give Lord Richly his discharge.

Herewith I dedicate myself to truth.
Fortune dispose me as you please.

12

The **Moderns'** *house.* **Mr Modern**, **Mrs Modern**. **Mr
Modern** *takes the twenty-pound note from* **Mrs Modern**.

Mr Modern
In short madam, you shall not drive a separate trade at my
expense.

Your person is mine: I bought it lawfully in the church
and unless I am to profit by the disposal
I shall keep it all for my own use.

Mrs Modern
This insolence is not to be borne.

Mr Modern
Have I not winked at all your intrigues?
Have I not pretended business to leave you and your gallants
together?
Have I not been the most obsequious observant . . .

Mrs Modern
Out with it; you know what you are.

Mr Modern
Do you upbraid me with your vices, madam?

Mrs Modern
My vices! Call it obedience to a husband's will.
Can you deny that you persuaded me to the undertaking?
Do you forget the arguments you used to convince me that
virtue was the lightest of bubbles?

Mr Modern
I own it all,
and if I felt the sweets of your pleasures, as I did at first,
I'd never once upbraid you with them,
but as I must share the dishonour
it is surely reasonable I should share the profit?

Mrs Modern
And have you not?

Mr Modern
What if I have?

Mrs Modern
Why do you complain then?

Mr Modern
Because I find those effects no more.
Your cards run away with the lucre of your other pleasures
and you lose to the knaves of your own sex
what you get from the fools of ours.

Mrs Modern
'Tis false, you know I seldom lose.
Nor indeed can I considerably,
for I have not, lately, had it in my power to stake high:
Lord Richly who was the fountain of our wealth hath long
been dry to me.

Mr Modern
I hope, madam, this new gallant will turn to a better
account.

Mrs Modern
Our amour is yet too young to expect any fruit from thence.

Mr Modern
I am sure if women sprung from the earth,
as some philosophers think,
it was from the clay of Egypt, not the sands of Peru.
Serpents and crocodiles are the only fruit they produce.

Mrs Modern
Very true, and a wife contains the whole ten plagues of her
country.

Mr Modern
Why had I not been a Turk
that I might have enslaved my wife;
or a Chinese that I might have sold her!

Mrs Modern
That would have been only the custom of the country;
you have done more, you have sold her in England;
in a country where women are as backward to be sold to a
lover as to refuse him;
and where cuckold is almost the only title of honour that
can't be bought.

Mr Modern
This ludicrous behaviour, madam,
as ill becomes the present subject
as entertaining new gallants doth the tenderness
you this morning expressed for your reputation.
In short it is impossible that your amours should be secret
long;
and however careless you have been of me

whilst I have had my horns in my pocket,
I hope you'll take care to gild them when I am to wear them
in public.

Mrs Modern
What would you have me do?

Mr Modern
Suffer me to discover you together
by which means we may make our fortunes easy all at once.
One good discovery in Westminster Hall will be of greater
service than his utmost generosity.
The law will give you more in one moment than his love for
many years.

Mrs Modern
Don't think of it.

Mr Modern
Yes, and resolve it; unless you agree to this, madam
then you must agree immediately to break up our house
and retire to the country.

Mrs Modern
Racks and tortures are in that name.

Mr Modern
But many more are in that of a prison:
so you must resolve either to quit the town or submit to my
reasons.

Mrs Modern
When reputation is gone all places are alike:
when I am despised in it I shall hate the town
as much as now I like it.

Mr Modern
There are other places and other towns;
the whole world is the house of the rich,
and they may live in what apartment they please.

Mrs Modern
I cannot resolve.

Mr Modern
But I can: if you will keep your reputation

you shall carry it into the country
where it will be of service – in town it is of none –
or if it be 'tis like clogs, only to those that walk on foot;
and the one will no more recommend you in an assembly
than the other.

Mrs Modern
You never had any love for me.

Mr Modern
Do you tax me with want of love for you?
Have I not for your sake stood the public mark of infamy?
Would you have had me poorly kept you, and starved you?
No I could not bear to see you want;
therefore have acted the part I've done:
and yet while I have winked at the giving up of your virtue
have I not been the most industrious to extol it everywhere?

Mrs Modern
So has Lord Richly and so have all his creatures,
a common trick among you,
to blazon out the reputation of women
whose virtue you have destroyed
and as industriously blacken them who have withstood you:
a deceit so stale that you commendation would sully a
woman of honour.

Mr Modern
I have no time to reason with you:
I shall leave you to consider on what I have said.

Exit **Mr Modern**.

Mrs Modern (*solas*)
Surely the happiest outcome
of these present events
would be if my husband
were taken to prison
then might I abscond with Bellamant?
But alas! I could never persuade him
to leave his wife.
How are my hopes frustrated.

Enter **Lord Richly**.

Lord Richly
What success my angel?

Mrs Modern
Expect all that lovers wish or husbands fear: she comes.

Lord Richly
When?

Mrs Modern
Now tonight, instantly.

Lord Richly
Thou glory of intrigue! What words shall thank thee?

Mrs Modern
No words at all my lord;
a hundred pounds must witness the first interview.

Lord Richly
They shall and if she yields, a thousand.

Mrs Modern
That you must not expect yet.

Lord Richly
By Heaven I do;
I have more reason to expect it than you imagine.
Since I left you Fortune seems to have watched for me.
I got her to piquet, threw away six parties
and left her a banknote of a hundred for the payment of six
pounds.

Mrs Modern
And did she receive it?

Lord Richly
With the same reluctance that a lawyer or physician would a
double fee, or a court-priest a plurality.

Mrs Modern
Then there is hope of success indeed.

Lord Richly
Hope? There is certainty: the next attempt must carry her.

Mrs Modern
You have a hundred friends in the garrison my lord.

Lord Richly
And if some of them do not open the gates for me,
the devil's in it.
I have succeeded often by leaving money in a lady's hands:
she spends it, is unable to pay and then I,
by virtue of my mortgage,
immediately enter upon the premises.

Mrs Modern
You are very generous, my lord.

Lord Richly
My money shall always be the humble servant of my
pleasures
and it is the interest of men of fortune to keep up the price of
beauty,
that they may have it more among themselves.

Mrs Modern
I am as much pleased as surprised at this your prospect of
success
and from this day forward I will think with you
all virtue to be only pride, caprice, and the fear of shame.

Lord Richly
Virtue, like the Ghost in *Hamlet*,
is here, there, every where and no where at all:
its appearance is as imaginary as that of a ghost;
and they are much the same sort of people
who are in love with one
and afraid of the other.
It is a ghost which hath seldom haunted me
but I had the power of laying it.

Mrs Modern
Yes my lord, I am a fatal instance of that power.

Lord Richly
And the dearest I assure you,
which is some sacrifice to your vanity;
and shortly I will make an offering to your revenge –
the two darling passions of your sex.

Mrs Modern
But how is it possible for me to leave you together
without the most abrupt rudeness?

Lord Richly
Never regard that as my success is sure,
she will hereafter thank you for a rudeness so seasonable.

Mrs Modern
Mr Bellamant too will be with her.

Lord Richly
He will be as agreeably entertained with you in the next
room;
and as he does not suspect the least design in me
he will be satisfied with my being in her company.

Mrs Modern
Sure you will not attempt his wife while he is in the house.

Lord Richly
Pish! He is in dependence on my interest,
so that rather than forfeit my favour
he would be himself her pander.
I have made twenty such men subscribe themselves cuckolds
by the prospect of one place which not one of them ever had.

Mrs Modern
So that your fools are not caught like the fish in the water by
a bait
but like the dog in the water by a shadow.

Lord Richly
Besides I may find a pretence of sending him away.

Mrs Modern
Go then to the chocolate-house
and leave a servant to bring you word of their arrival.
It will be better you should come in to them than they find
you here.

Lord Richly
I will be guided by you in all things
and be assured the consummation of my wishes
shall be the success of your own.

Exit **Lord Richly**.

Mrs Modern
That they shall indeed, though in a way you little imagine.
This forwardness of Mrs Bellamant's meets my swiftest
wishes.
Could I once give Bellamant reason to suspect his wife
then I would despair not of the happiest effect of his passion
for me.
Ha! He's here and alone.

Enter **Mr Bellamant**.

Mrs Modern
Where's Mrs Bellamant?

Mr Bellamant
She shall be here immediately.
But I chose a few moments' privacy with you;
first to deliver this,
(*He gives her the hundred-pound note again.*)
and next to ask you one question,
which do not be startled at.
Pray how did you employ that note you received this
morning?

Mrs Modern
Nay, if you expect an account of me,
let me return you this.

Mr Bellamant
Do not so injuriously mistake me.
Nothing but the most extraordinary reason could force me to
ask you;
know then that the very note you had of me this morning,
I received within this hour from my wife.

Mrs Modern *laughs and returns the note.*

Mr Bellamant
Why do you laugh madam?

Mrs Modern
Out of triumph, to see what empty politicians men are found
when they oppose their weak heads to ours!
On my conscience a parliament of women would be of great
service to the nation.

Mr Bellamant
Were all ladies capable as you Mrs Modern, I should be
ready to vote on your side.

Mrs Modern
Nay, nay sir, you must not leave out your wife
especially you that have the best wife in the world!

Mr Bellamant
Forgive me, madam, if I have been too partial to a woman
whose whole business hath been to please me.

Mrs Modern
Oh! You have no reason to be ashamed of your good
opinion;
you are not singular in it I assure you;
Mrs Bellamant will have more votes than one.

Mr Bellamant
I am indifferent how many she has
since I am sure she will make interest but for one.

Mrs Modern
It is the curse of fools to be secure.

Mr Bellamant
I cannot guess your meaning.

Mrs Modern
Then to introduce my explanation,
the note you lent me I lost at piquet to Lord Richly.

Mr Bellamant
To Lord Richly!

Mrs Modern
Who perhaps might dispose of it to someone
who might lend it to others who might give it to those
who might lose it to your wife.

Mr Bellamant (*aside*)
Is this why she would not tell me where she got it?

(*To* **Mrs Modern**.) I know not what to suppose.

Mrs Modern
Nor I, for sure one cannot suppose,

especially since you have the best wife in the world;
one cannot suppose
that it could be a present from Lord Richly to herself;
that she received it;
that in return she hath an assignation to meet him here.

Mr Bellamant
Suppose! Hell and damnation! No.

Mrs Modern
But certainly one could not affirm that this is truth.

Mr Bellamant
Affirm?

Mrs Modern
And yet all this is true, as true as she is false.
Nay you shall have an instance;
an immediate undeniable instance.
You shall see it with your own eyes and hear it with your
own ears.

Mr Bellamant
Am I alive?

Mrs Modern
If all the husbands of these best wives in the world are dead
we are a strange nation of ghosts.
If you will be prudent and be like the rest of your brethren,
keep the affair secret; I assure you I'll never discover it.

Mr Bellamant
Secret! Yes, as inward fire till sure destruction shall attend
its blaze.
But why do I rage? It is impossible, she must be innocent.

Mrs Modern
Then Lord Richly is a greater villain to belie that innocence
to me.
But give yourself no pain since you are shortly to be certain.
Go fetch her hither, Lord Richly will be here almost as soon
as you:
then feign some excuse to leave the room, I will follow you,
and convey you where you shall have an opportunity of
being a witness
either to her innocence or her guilt.

Mr Bellamant
This goodness, my sweetest creature, shall bind me yours for ever.

Mrs Modern
To convince you that is all I desire
I am willing to leave the town and my reputation at once
and retire with you wherever you please.

Mr Bellamant
That must be the subject of our future thoughts.
How can I think of anything else now but satisfaction in this affair?

Exit **Mr Bellamant**.

Mrs Modern (*aside*)
Does he demur to my offer?
The villain.
When my husband is confined to a cell
how shall I live
without Bellamant to support me?
Am I to be only the momentary object
of his looser pleasures
while his wife yet sits nearest his heart?
I dare not conceive what
the future might disclose to me as a woman alone.
Perhaps he will change his mind
once Richly has seduced her?
The stakes could not be higher,
all my hopes are in the balance
and the hour approaches that shall decide my fate for ever.

13

At the **Moderns'** *house later.* **Lord Richly**, **Mr Bellamant**,
Mrs Bellamant, **Mrs Modern**.

Lord Richly (*to* **Mrs Bellamant**)
Well, madam, you have drawn a most delightful sketch of life.

Mrs Modern
Then it is 'still life', for I dare swear there never were such
people breathing.

Mrs Bellamant (*aside*)
Miss Impudence!

(*To* **Mrs Modern**.) Don't you believe then, madam,
it is possible for a married couple to be happy in one another
without desiring any other company?

Mrs Modern (*aside*)
Miss Bitchington!

(*To* **Mrs Bellamant**.) Indeed I do not know how it may have
been in the plains of Arcadia; but truly in those of Great
Britain I believe not.

Lord Richly
I must subscribe to that too.

Mrs Bellamant
Mr Bellamant, what say you?

Mr Bellamant
Oh, my dear I am entirely of your mind.
(*Aside*.) What else could I say here?

Lord Richly
This is a miracle almost equal to the other,
to see a husband and wife of the same opinion.
I must be a convert too,
for it would be the greatest miracle of all to find Mrs
Bellamant in the wrong.

Mrs Bellamant
It would be a much greater to find want of compliance in
Lord Richly.

Mr Bellamant (*aside*)
What?

Mrs Modern
Nay, madam, this is hardly so
for I have heard his lordship say the same in your absence.

Mrs Modern *kicks* **Mr Bellamant**.

Lord Richly
Dear Bellamant,
I believe I have had an opportunity to serve you this
afternoon.
I have spoken to Lord Powerful,
he says he is willing to do for you.
Sir Peter they tell me is given over
and I fancy you may find my lord at home now.

Mr Bellamant
I must take another opportunity, my lord,
a particular affair now preventing me.

Lord Richly
I must advise you as a friend:
the loss of an hour hath been the loss of a place.
Unless that is you have something of greater consequence.

Mr Bellamant
Be assured. I shall find a method of thanking you.

Mrs Modern (*aside to* **Mr Bellamant**)
Make this a handle to slip out,
I'll come into the next room to you.

Mr Bellamant
My lord, I am much obliged to your friendship.
My dear, I'll call you in my return:
Mrs Modern, I am your humble servant.

Lord Richly
I wish you success, you may command any thing in my
power to forward it.

Mr Bellamant *exits*.

Mrs Bellamant
Mr Bellamant is more indebted to your lordship than he will
be ever able to pay.

Lord Richly
Mr Bellamant, madam, has a friend,
who is able to pay more obligations than I can lay on him.

Mrs Modern (*to* **Mrs Bellamant**)
Will you forgive me if I am forced to be guilty of a piece of
rudeness by leaving you one moment too?

Mrs Modern *exits*.

Lord Richly (*aside*)
And I shall not be guilty of losing it.

Mrs Bellamant (*aside*)
What can this mean?

Mrs Modern *and* **Mr Bellamant** *spy upon* **Lord Richly** *and* **Mrs Bellamant**.

Lord Richly
And can you, madam, think of retiring from the general admiration of mankind?

Mrs Bellamant
With pleasure, my lord to the particular admiration of him who is to me all mankind.

Lord Richly *begins to extinguish the candles*.

Mr Bellamant (*aside*)
What shall I spy here?
What did I hope?
What do I wish to see?

Mrs Modern
Sssh . . .

Lord Richly (*to* **Mrs Bellamant**)
Is it possible any man can be so happy?

Mrs Bellamant
I hope my lord you think Mr Bellamant so.

Lord Richly
If he be, I pity him less for his losses
than I envy him the love of her
in whose power it may be to redress them.

Mr Bellamant (*aside*)
What shall I do if she succumbs?

Mrs Modern
Fly away with me my love?

Mrs Bellamant (*to* **Lord Richly**)
You surprise me my lord: how in my power?

Lord Richly
Whatever is in the power of man is in yours:
I am sure what little assistance mine can give is readily at
your devotion.

Mr Bellamant (*aside*)
Why do I not speak out now?
Why am I silent here?

Mrs Modern
Ssssh!

She kisses him.

Lord Richly
My interest and fortune are all in these dear hands;
in short madam
I have languished a long time for an opportunity
to tell you that I have the most violent passion for you.

Mrs Bellamant *snatches the last candle*.

Mrs Bellamant
My lord I have been unwilling to understand you
but now your expression leaves me no other doubt
but whether I hate or despise you most.

Lord Richly
Are these the ungrateful returns you give my love?

Mrs Bellamant
Is this the friendship you have professed to Mr Bellamant?

Lord Richly
I'll make his fortune.
Let this be an instance of my future favours.

He puts a banknote in her hand. She throws it away.

Mrs Bellamant
And this of my reception of them.
Be assured my lord if you ever renew this unmannerly attack
on my honour I will be revenged, my husband shall know his
obligations to you.

Lord Richly
I have gone too far to retreat madam!

If I cannot be the object of your love let me be obliged to
your prudence.
How many families are supported by this method which you
start at?
Does not many a woman in this town drive her husband's
coach?

Mrs Bellamant
My lord this insolence is intolerable;
and from this hour I never will see your face again.

A noise without. **Mrs Bellamant** *accidentally extinguishes the
candle.*

Lord Richly
What is the meaning of this?

Mr Modern (*off*)
Come out strumpet, show thy face and thy adulterer's before
the world;
thou shalt be an example of the vengeance of an injured
husband.

Lord Richly (*aside*)
I have no farther business here at present,
for I fear more husbands have discovered injuries than one.

Lord Richly *escapes out of the window.* **Mr Modern** *enters with
a lantern and a sword and reveals* **Mrs Modern** *and* **Mr
Bellamant**, *where they are concealed.*

Mrs Bellamant
Protect me Heavens! What do I see!

Mr Bellamant
This was a masterpiece of my evil genius.

Mrs Modern
Sir this insult upon my reputation shall not go unrevenged,
I have brothers who will defend their sister's fame
from the base attacks of a perfidious husband,
from any shame he would bring on her innocence.

Mr Modern
Thou hast a forehead that would defend itself from any
shame

but for what you have grafted on my forehead,
I must thank you and this worthy gentleman.

Mrs Modern
Sir, you shall smart for the faleshood of this accusation.

Mr Modern
Madam, you shall smart for your dishonour.

Mrs Modern
'Your dishonour'? My dishonour?

Mr Modern
My dishonour.

Mrs Modern
Our dishonour?

Mr Modern
Your dishonour is our dishonour is my dishonour!
(*To* **Bellamant**.) And as for you, sir,
you may depend upon it
I shall take the strictest satisfaction
which the law will give me,
so I shall leave you at present
to give satisfaction to your wife.

Mr Modern *picks up the banknote and exits.*

Mr Bellamant (*after some pause*)
When the criminal turns his own accuser,
the merciful judge becomes his advocate;
guilt is too plainly written in my face to admit of a denial,
and I stand prepared to receive what sentence you please.

Mrs Bellamant
As you are your own accuser, be your own judge;
you can inflict no punishment on yourself
equal to what I feel.

Mr Bellamant
Death has no terrors equal to that thought.
Ha! I have involved thee in my ruin,
and thou must be the wretched partaker of my misfortune.

Mrs Bellamant
While I was assured of your truth

I could have thought that happiness enough;
yet I have still this to comfort me,
the same moment that has betrayed your guilt
has discovered my innocence.

Mr Bellamant (*to himself*)
Oh! thou ungrateful fool,
what stores of bliss hast thou in one moment destroyed!
Oh! my angel, how have I requited all your love and
goodness?
For what have I forsaken thy tender virtuous passion?

Mrs Bellamant
For a new one. How could I be so easily deceived?
How could I imagine there was such truth in man,
in that inconstant fickle sex, who are so prone to change;
that, to indulge their fondness for variety,
they would grow weary of a paradise to wander in a desert?

Mr Bellamant
How weak is that comparison to show the difference between
thee and every other woman!

Mrs Bellamant
I had once that esteem of you;
but hereafter I shall think all men the same;
and when I have weaned myself of love for you,
will hate them all alike.

Mr Bellamant
Thy sentence is too just.
I own I have deserved it; I never merited so good a wife.
Heaven saw it had given too much
and thus has taken the blessing from me.

Mrs Bellamant
You will soon think otherwise.
If absence from me can bring you to those thoughts
I am resolved to favour them.

Mr Bellamant
Thou shalt enjoy thy wish;
we will part, part this night, this hour.
Yet let me ask one favour:

the ring which was a witness of our meeting,
let it be so of our separation.

She returns to him her wedding ring.

Let me bear this as a memorial of our love.
This shall remind me of the tender moments we have had
together,
and serve to aggravate my sorrows:
henceforth I'll study only to be miserable;
let Heaven make you happy and curse me as it pleases.

Mrs Bellamant
It cannot make thee more wretched than you have made me.

Mr Bellamant
Yet, do believe me when I say
I never injured you with any other woman.
Nay believe me when I swear,
how much soever I may deserve the shame I suffer,
I did not now deserve it.

Mrs Modern (*to* **Mrs Bellamant**)
If I were to speak
I see no reason
why you should credit
any word I might utter.
But yet I beg you leave . . .

Mrs Bellamant
Madam, I have no quarrel with you.

Mrs Modern
I will not deny what has passed
betwixt he and I.
The money he borrowed from you
was at my request.
When I lost it at piquet to Lord Richly
and then received it a second time from your husband,
I suggested that he might have reason to suspect you.
He would not contemplate it.
I told him the truth would be discovered here tonight,
and now it is,
yet not as any of us expected.
I am your rival no more.

Mrs Bellamant
Mrs Modern, your candour illuminates
this darkest hour of night.

Exit **Mrs Modern**.

Mrs Bellamant
And must we part?

Mr Bellamant
Since it obliges you.

Mrs Bellamant
That I may have nothing to remember you by,
take back this, and this, and this,
and all the thousand embraces thou hast given me —
till I die in thy loved arms —
and thus we part for ever.

Mr Bellamant
Ha!
Without you, life is what I have no reason to be fond of
and a grave appears to me the happiest and best retreat.
Should you ever find it in your heart to forgive me,
even if I were at the furthest end of the earth,
I would come running.

Mrs Bellamant
I cannot now forgive you the fault
that has been revealed this night
— and the reason is, because I have forgiven it long ago.
Here, my dear (*Producing* **Mrs Modern***'s letter.*)
is an instance that I am likewise capable
of keeping a secret.
Forget it as a frightful dream.
It is no more.

Mr Bellamant
Oh! Let me press thee to my heart;
for every moment that I hold thee thus
gives bliss beyond expression;
a bliss no vice can give. Now life appears desirable again.
Yet shall I not see thee miserable?
Shall I not see my children suffer for their father's crime?

Mrs Bellamant
Indulge no more uneasy thoughts;
fortune may have blessings yet in store for us and them.
Do you know that I have laid down the prettiest scheme
for matrimony that ever entered into the taste of people of
condition?

Mr Bellamant
Oh pray let's hear it!

Mrs Bellamant
In the first place then,
I am resolved positively to be mistress of myself,
I must have my chamber to myself,
my coach to myself,
my servants to myself,
my table-time and company to myself.
Nay, and sometimes,
when I have the mind to be out of humour,
my bed to myself.
Finally and above all
I must have you to myself.

Mr Bellamant
Excellent goodness!
My future days shall have no labour but for thy happiness;
and from this hour I'll never give thee cause of a complaint.

Mrs Bellamant
When but two the world possessed,
'Twas their happiest days, and best.

Mr Bellamant
And whatsoever rocks the fates may lay
In life's hard passage to obstruct our way,
Patient the toilsome journey I'll abide!
And bless my fortune with so dear a guide.

He replaces the wedding ring on her finger.

14

Next morning. **Lord Richly**, **Mr Bellamant**.

Lord Richly (*aside*)
What can the meaning of this be?
Perhaps he comes to make proposals concerning his wife;
but love shall not get the better of my reason
as to lead me to an extravagant price,
I'll not go above two thousand, that's positive.

Mr Bellamant
My lord, I have received an obligation from you which I
return.

Gives him the hundred-pound note.

Lord Richly
Pshaw! Trifles of this nature can hardly be called
obligations,
I would do twenty times as much for dear Jack Bellamant.

Mr Bellamant
The obligation was to my wife,
nor hath she made you a small return,
since it is to her entreaty you owe your present safety.

Lord Richly
I am not apprised of any danger,
but would owe my safety to none sooner
than Mrs Bellamant.

Mr Bellamant
Come, come my lord, this prevarication is low and mean;
you know you have used me basely,
and under the cover of friendship
have attempted to corrupt my wife,
for which, but that I would not suffer the least breath of
scandal to sully her reputation,
I would exact such vengeance on thee –

Lord Richly
Sir, I must acquaint you that this is a language I have not
been used to.

Mr Bellamant
No, the language of flatterers and hireling sycophants
is what you are used to,
wretches whose honour and love are as venal as their praise.

Such your title might awe or your fortune bribe to silence;
such you should have dealt with
and not have dared to injure a man of honour.

Lord Richly
This is such presumption.

Mr Bellamant
No, my lord, yours was the presumption,
mine is only justice, nay and mild too,
unequal to your crime
which requires a punishment from my hand
not from my tongue.

Lord Richly
Do you consider who I am?

Mr Bellamant
Were you as high as heraldry could lift you,
you should not injure me unpunished.
Where grandeur can give licence to oppression
the people must be slaves,
let them boast what liberty they please.

Lord Richly
Sir, you shall hear of this.

Mr Bellamant
I shall be ready to justify my words
by any action you dare provoke me to
and be assured of this,
if ever I discover any future attempt of yours to my
dishonour
your life shall be its sacrifice.
Henceforward let us behave as if we had never met.

Exit **Mr Bellamant**.

Lord Richly
Here's your man of sense now,
half ruined in the House of Lord a few days ago
and in a fair way of going the other step in Westminster Hall
in a few days more;
yet he has the impudence to threaten a man of my fortune
and quality

for attempting to debauch his wife,
which many a fool who rides in his coach and six
would have had sense enough to have winked at.

15

Mr Bellamant, **Mrs Modern**.

Mr Bellamant
This is exactly the time I appointed her to meet me here.
Ha! She comes.
You are punctual as a young lover to a first appointment.

Mrs Modern
Women commonly begin to be punctual when men leave off:
our passions seldom reach their meridian before yours set.

Mr Bellamant
We can no more help the decrease of our passions
than you the increase of yours.
And though like the sun,
I was obliged to quit your atmosphere,
you have left a moon to shine in it.

Mrs Modern
Oh Bellamant! I am undone and it is plain I have no longer
any share in your love.

Mr Bellamant
Blame not my inconstancy but your own.

Mrs Modern
By all our joys I never loved another.

Mr Bellamant
Will you deny your favours to Lord Richly?

Mrs Modern
He makes love to every woman he sees,
neither the strictest friendship preferred to her husband,
nor the best reputation on her side,
can preserve any woman he likes from his attacks:
for he is arrived at a happy way of regarding
all the rest of mankind as his tenants,

and thinks, because he possesses more than they,
he is entitled to whatever they possess.
He had my person but you alone had my heart.

Mr Bellamant
I have always taken a woman's person to be the strongest
assurance of her heart.

Mrs Modern
Thou ass to think that the heart of a woman
is to be won by gold as well as her person;
but you will find that though a woman often sells her person,
she always gives her heart.

Mr Bellamant
I think the love of a mistress who gives up her person
is no more to be doubted than the love of a friend who gives
up his purse.

Mrs Modern
By Heavens, I hate Richly equally with my husband,
and as I was forced to marry the latter
by the commands of my parents
so was I given up to the former
by the entreaties of my husband.
Hell and his blacker soul doth know the truth of what I say:
that he betrayed me first
and has ever since been the pander of our amour.
To you my own inclination led me.
Lord Richly was my husband's choice
but you alone were mine.

Mr Bellamant
Why do you voice these sentiments?
Do you not know why I called you here?
It was to say goodbye.

Mrs Modern
Goodbye?

Mr Bellamant
We go into the country today.
I have repented now.
So farewell.

Mr Bellamant *exits.*

Mrs Modern (*solas*)
You see where I am now?

I shall not pursue repentance in the lonely woods,
not when the town is crammed
with rakes and fops and sparks and beaus!
What is life without another drink,
another dress, another dance,
a masquerade or a game of cards?
Who wants to be virtuous, and old?
I should rather gamble with my life.
· You see how I am now?
You will not redeem me.
Above all do not pity me.
You shall not know what will become of me.

17

Lord Richly, **Mr Modern**. **Lord Richly** *giving* **Mr Modern**
the hundred-pound note.

Mr Modern
My lord I am honoured with your favours.
Now I have just enough to pay the summons
and 'scape detention in a prison cell.

Lord Richly
I am concerned for your misfortune, Mr Modern.

Mr Modern
I understand now why you warned me of Mr Bellamant.
He has robbed me of the affections of a wife
whom I loved as tenderly as myself.
Forgive my tears my lord –
I have lost all I held dear in this world.

Lord Richly
Comfort yourself with hopes of revenge.

Mr Modern
Alas!
My lord, what revenge can equal the dishonour
she has brought upon my family?

Think on that, my lord, on the dishonour I must endure.
I cannot name the title they will give me.

Lord Richly
It is shocking indeed.
Laws cannot be too rigorous against offences of this nature:
juries cannot give too great damages.

Mr Modern
My ease for ever lost, my quiet gone;
my honour, my lord.
Oh 'tis a tender wound.

Lord Richly
In cases of this nature
even friendship itself must be thrown up.
Injuries of this kind are not to be forgiven.
To attempt the wife of a friend
to what wickedness will men arrive?

Mr Modern
I see it differently my lord,
it is a common misfortune to have a bad wife.

Lord Richly
Though dear Jack Bellamant be my particular friend
I cannot persuade you from the most vigorous prosecution.

Mr Modern
But I cannot prosecute without an independent witness
and there was none other present who might testify.
Was there, my lord?

Lord Richly
True. That is indeed a pity.

Mr Modern
Mrs Bellamant cannot be asked to testify against her
husband.

Lord Richly
No?

Mr Modern
Look at it this way:
If someone were to have attempted Mrs Bellamant's virtue
that night,

and Mr Bellamant were to prosecute that individual,
and if I and my wife were prepared to swear witness
to the event,
then he would have a case.

Lord Richly
My dear friend, I fail to understand your meaning.

Mr Modern
My lord, I am unable to prosecute Mr Bellamant
for lack of a witness,
but if the circumstances were different
if it were his wife's reputation that was assaulted
by some other individual
then he could find witnesses.

Lord Richly
But there was no other individual present?

Mr Modern
Yes, that's what I said my lord.

Lord Richly
So?

Mr Modern
Is it not my good fortune
that while I sacrifice the pursuit of damages
I may enjoy your lordship's munificent generosity?

Lord Richly
Humph! (*Aside.*) Scab!

Mr Modern
. . . While I forgo the opportunity of revenge,
I can rely upon my true friend
to procure some effortless and well-paid employment
that I may restore my self-respect?

Lord Richly
Mr Modern, you give me no choice, I am your servant.

Mr Modern
Thank you my lord.

Lord Richly's *Epilogue*.

Lord Richly
To speak a bold truth:
I am inclined to suspect that the public voice
hath done much injustice to Fortune
and hath convicted her of many facts
in which she had not the least concern.
I question whether we may not by Natural Means
account for all the miseries
which men and women of sense involve themselves
by quitting the directions of prudence:
in short for all the phenomena
which are imputed to Fortune,
whom perhaps men accuse with no less absurdity in life
than a bad player complains of ill luck at a game of cards?

Methuen Modern Plays

include work by

Jean Anouilh	Larry Kramer
John Arden	Stephen Lowe
Margaretta D'Arcy	Doug Lucie
Peter Barnes	John McGrath
Brendan Behan	David Mamet
Edward Bond	Arthur Miller
Bertolt Brecht	Mtwa, Ngema & Simon
Howard Brenton	Tom Murphy
Simon Burke	Peter Nichols
Jim Cartwright	Joe Orton
Caryl Churchill	Louise Page
Noël Coward	Luigi Pirandello
Sarah Daniels	Stephen Poliakoff
Nick Dear	Franca Rame
Shelagh Delaney	Philip Ridley
David Edgar	David Rudkin
Dario Fo	Willy Russell
Michael Frayn	Jean-Paul Sartre
Paul Godfrey	Sam Shepard
John Guare	Wole Soyinka
Peter Handke	C. P. Taylor
Declan Hughes	Theatre Workshop
Terry Johnson	Sue Townsend
Kaufman & Hart	Timberlake Wertenbaker
Barrie Keeffe	Victoria Wood

Methuen World Classics

Aeschylus (two volumes)
Jean Anouilh
John Arden (two volumes)
Arden & D'Arcy
Aristophanes (two volumes)
Aristophanes & Menander
Peter Barnes (two volumes)
Brendan Behan
Aphra Behn
Edward Bond (four volumes)
Bertolt Brecht
  (four volumes)
Howard Brenton
  (two volumes)
Büchner
Bulgakov
Calderón
Anton Chekhov
Caryl Churchill
  (two volumes)
Noël Coward (five volumes)
Sarah Daniels (two volumes)
Eduardo De Filippo
David Edgar (three volumes)
Euripides (three volumes)
Dario Fo (two volumes)
Michael Frayn (two volumes)
Max Frisch
Gorky
Harley Granville Barker
  (two volumes)
Henrik Ibsen (six volumes)

Terry Johnson
Lorca (three volumes)
David Mamet
Marivaux
Mustapha Matura
David Mercer
  (two volumes)
Arthur Miller
  (four volumes)
Anthony Minghella
Molière
Tom Murphy
  (three volumes)
Peter Nichols (two volumes)
Clifford Odets
Joe Orton
Louise Page
A. W. Pinero
Luigi Pirandello
Stephen Poliakoff
  (two volumes)
Terence Rattigan
Ntozake Shange
Sophocles (two volumes)
Wole Soyinka
David Storey (two volumes)
August Strindberg
  (three volumes)
J. M. Synge
Ramón del Valle-Inclán
Frank Wedekind
Oscar Wilde

Methuen Student Editions